John L. Tomkinson has a Bachelors degree in Theology and Philosophy from St. David's College, Lampeter, (University of Wales); an MA and a PhD in Philosophy, and another MA in History, all from the University of Keele.

He has lived in Greece since 1985, where he prepares students for international university entrance examinations in History and the Theory of Knowledge at a large Greek private school. He writes educational books and books about Greece.

Cover Design: Aliki Kotsikou

Between Heaven and Earth

The Greek Church

John L. Tomkinson

Anagnosis
Athens

Anagnosis
Harilaou Trikoupi 130
145 63 Kifissia
Athens, Greece
Tel.++30 210 6254 654
Fax ++30 210 6254 089
Website: www.anagnosis.gr

ISBN 960-87186-5-1

Photoset by:
Alphabeto A.E.B.E.
Digeni Akrita 13
114 72 Athens
www.alphabet.gr
Printed and bound by:
K. Pletsas - Z. Karadri O.E.
Harilaou Trikoupi 107
Athens
www.typografio.gr

Preface

The immediate spur for the writing of this book was the author's surprise and annoyance at hearing some tourists in the Plaka district of Athens (clearly "born-again" Christians from the far side of the Atlantic) commenting contemptuously on a Greek priest, distinguished by his characteristic beard, stove pipe hat and black robes, who happened to be passing. They were clearly quite unconscious of the irony of the situation. Not only were they supremely confident in their own possession of the Fully-Revealed Truth, which they had apparently obtained from their personal reading of Scripture, but they also betrayed an almost total lack of knowledge of the origins of their own faith, and were bereft of any historical perspective. They were not quite as bad as the grandfather of a friend from the Mid-West of the United States, who demanded to know why his grandson should do something so bizarre as to learn French, on the curious grounds that "English was good enough for Jesus Christ." Just as my friend's grandfather evidently thought that the historical Jesus spoke English - the English of the King James' Bible, incidentally - so these visitors to Greece seemed to be under the impression that the New Testament was immediately accessible and open to them in English, without any knowledge of the linguistic and cultural background from which it had emerged. They simply assumed that if Greeks thought and behaved differently from themselves, this showed the distance of the benighted Greeks from the Full Truth.

They seemed to have no inkling that their own faith is but a recent fragmentary offshoot of a tradition which was a consequence of cultural intercourse between the Semitic and Greek intellectual worlds within the Roman super-state. They seemed to have no idea that the conceptual world of the New Testament was expressed in the language of the very people they denigrated. They obviously did not know that the church council which made the decision about which books to include within the New Testament, and which to exclude, was a synod of the Greek Church of Laodicea in 367. They were not aware that the chief contents of the faith to which they adhered so dogmatically were hammered out in a series of ecumenical councils by the very bishops of the Church which they derided. They did not know that the tradition to which the intellectual and spiritual collision between the Semitic and Greek worlds gave birth is still flourishing in unbroken cultural and social continuity today – and that it was precisely this to which, in their ignorance, they so confidently felt superior.

By contrast, in *The Waters of Marah* Peter Hammond recalled the overwhelming impression made upon a much better-educated Russian friend when he first visited Greece: "He had travelled by train from Paris, and at the Greek frontier a *douanier* boarded the train to greet him and his companion with the very salutation wherewith the risen Lord had greeted His wondering disciples on the first Easter morning."[1]

5

Historian Arnold Toynbee writes: "Among all the Christian churches that are in existence today, the Greek-speaking branches of the Eastern Orthodox Church are unique in possessing the whole original corpus of Christian religious literature, and the whole of the Eastern Orthodox liturgy too, in the Attic *koine* in which this literature was inherited by the Christians (as it was in the case of the Old Testament) or was written by them (as was the New)." Thus, "The humblest peasant who reads his Septuagint and New Testament on the hills of Boeotia may proudly feel that he has an access to the original oracles of divine truth which Pope or Cardinal reaches by a barbarous and imperfect translation."[2]

The term "Greek Church" is an ambiguous one. The vast majority of the population of Greece belong to what is today called in the West "the Eastern Orthodox Church", an institution which has a greater claim than any other to historical continuity with the Church of the apostles. This so-called "Eastern" Church is in reality a federation of essentially independent bodies, bound together by a common faith and common traditional practices, in communion with the Ecumenical Patriarch of Constantinople.

One of the independent churches in this family is the Greek National Church. However, three considerations complicate what would appear at first sight to be a simple matter of identification. Firstly, the Ecumenical Patriarchate of Constantinople is itself also a Greek Church, in the sense at least that its traditions and rites are Byzantine, and its language Greek. Secondly, not all the local churches within the territorial boundaries of the modern Greek state fall under the jurisdiction of the Greek National Church. The islands of the Eastern Aegean and the monastic republic of Mount Athos are directly administered by the Ecumenical Patriarchate, while the status of Northern Greece (Epiros, Macedonia and Thrace) and Crete is somewhat ambiguous. Moreover, the national Church of Cyprus, a church which has enjoyed independence from all patriarchates from time immemorial, is also a Greek Church.

For purposes of this book, the term "Greek Church" will somewhat arbitrarily refer both to the Greek National Church and also to the Ecumenical Patriarchate, insofar as the latter is responsible for churches in the area of the modern Greek state.

This volume is intended to serve as a primary introduction to the Greek Church for Western visitors and others, written from the point of view of a sympathetic outsider. The first part consists of a description of the institutions, practices and faith of the Church as the visitor finds it today: its buildings, its worship, its organisation, its doctrines, etc. Since no institution is comprehensible without some knowledge of how and why it came to be as it is, the second part consists of a very brief summary of its eventful history.

John L. Tomkinson

Athens, 2003

Contents

Acknowledgements

My thanks are due to Aris Karey, Vicky Aggeli, Constantinos Aivalis, Marcus Debaca, Pamela Brown, Spyros Kasimatis and Despina Mouzaki. Photograph on page 52 courtesy and copyright of the Moraitis School, Athens. Illustrations on pp.10, 36, 54, 61, 68, 73-75, 77, 78, 84, 97, 106 and 149 are copyright of Eurokinisi. All the views expressed are the responsibility of the author alone.

Part One

Archbishop Christodoulos of "Athens and all Greece"
gives a blessing

1

Temples of Gold

One of the most striking characteristics of the Greek landscape is the distinctive style of the church buildings. Greek churches do not impress by their great length or height. They are, as Cecil Stewart points out, buildings "of mass, not lines". The whole ... is intrinsically tied together in complete structural unity."[1] It is often said that whereas the large Gothic buildings of the West strain upwards to reach the heavens, Greek churches, by contrast, seek to bring heaven down upon earth. Greek churches are frequently surprisingly small and homely to Westerners, but their painted walls and icons surround the believer with glowing representations of the inhabitants of heaven.

The Development of the Byzantine Style

The first purpose-built churches were erected in the style of the Roman basilica, a building designed for civic activities and functions, especially those of a lawcourt. As was always their custom, the ancient Romans developed a standard functional pattern which could be used throughout their empire. It was a rectangular hall divided into three aisles by interior colonnades, with either one or three semicircular apses at the end opposite the main entrance. Such buildings usually had tiled, sloping roofs. Some ancient church buildings of the simple basilican type still survive, and are still used by Greek Christians, of which the most famous and oldest is probably the Church of the Nativity in Bethlehem, built over the traditional site of the cave-stable where Jesus was born.

The earliest basilicas adopted for use by Christians were not oriented, but by the fourth or fifth century they were usually built with the apse at the east end and the main entrance at the west, so that the worshippers faced east, and the rising sun.

Single hemispherical apse of small church

11

Already, by the fourth or fifth century, the Church had begun to adapt something of the ceremonious style of the Roman state in its own rituals, which increasingly required a splendid setting. At that time, it was felt that this could best be achieved by placing a dome over the centre of the basilica. This would at the same time increase both the volume of space and the amount of light inside the building. But to build a dome over a basilica required the solution of a difficult practical problem.

It was comparatively easy to place a dome over a circular building, and this had been done several times in the ancient world, for example, in the Pantheon at Rome. The problem was how to suspend a dome, with its circular base, over a rectangular or square building. Over the course of time, two different methods were devised. One was to build a series of small relieving arches, known as squinches, spanning each angle of the square, to form an octagon, on which the dome could be built. A more elegant alternative was the use of pendentives: curved triangles rising from the corners of the square base, and gradually bending into the hemisphere of the dome.

The church of Ayia Sophia, Constantinople

The apotheosis of this style of architecture was achieved in 537, with the consecration of the great church of Ayia Sophia in Constantinople. Frequently described as a "miracle in space", this huge church was built within seven years, on the orders of the emperor Justinian. This is said to have been achieved by one hundred foremen each with one hundred men working for him. The walls at the sides are buttressed by high transepts with half domes, to allow them to bear the stress of the huge central dome, so that the whole is cruciform in shape.

Ayia Sophia became, in the minds of Christians, the ideal church building, and a pattern for all others throughout the empire. Thus there arose the classic Byzantine Greek church architectural style, based upon a cross-shaped building with equal transepts, or arms, surmounted by a dome, which may, or may not, be suspended on a tall cylindrical drum.

Despite a fundamental unity of conception, Byzantine architecture by no means remained static. On the basis of the original schema, buildings of great architectural complexity have been erected.

In particular, and probably under the influence of Armenian architects, in order to support the stress of the dome, the angles of the cross frequently came to be filled in by lower roofed sections. In time, bell towers might also be added.

A Byzantine church is designed primarily to be viewed from the inside rather than the outside. Nevertheless, the exteriors were sometimes decorated by patterns made out of different types of bricks, or even with masonry taken from older buildings.

Sometimes the outside of a church may be decorated with frescos or mosaics. This is particularly likely over the main entrance.

Since the area now part of the Greek state was a small part of the wider Greek world during the Byzantine period, and Athens a provincial university town subjected to repeated attacks and invasions, older churches are usually very small, and dwarfed by modern concrete office blocks.

Above: Top: Ayias Nikolaos, Serres   Middle : Panayitsa, Kifissia
Bottom: Ayios Ioannis Pelika, Maroussi
Below Left: Ay Thodoros, Athens   Below Rright: Omorphi ekklesia, Galatsi

Only some time after achieving independence was it possible to build larger churches. The church of Ayias Dimitrios, Kifissia,*(opposite)* is typical of the larger town centre churches erected during the late nineteenth and earlier twentieth centuries.

Recent years have seen a period of intensive church building, to cater to the new suburbs. Concrete is liberally employed as the chief building material, although it is frequently disguised in some way. The use of reinforced concrete has obvious advantages in a seismically active region. It also has the effect of freeing the more adventurous architects to experiment with new, and sometimes surprising, variations on the traditional style.

Bells and Planks

In order to alert the congregation to the performance of service early Christians used a long plank of wood or sheet of metal struck with a hammer. This device, known as a *semantron*, which may be carried on the shoulder or suspended from a ceiling or frame, is still employed in monastic churches in Greece, and may occasionally be found hanging outside some older, non-monastic buildings. Only later did the more familiar bell made its appearance. The use of these was banned throughout most of Greece under Turkish rule, which may go some way to explaining their great popularity today.

The bells belonging to Greek churches are generally smaller than those used in Western Europe, and may be hung from simple frames outside the church, or in towers. The latter may be constructed separately from the church itself. Today, in the cities the bells are often rung electrically.

Outside a Greek church a small kiosk on a raised platform may sometimes be seen. This is used for several ceremonies which take place outside the building, such as the proclamation of the Resurrection at midnight on Easter Day, and for the blessing of the water at Theofanio. *(Above)*

Many churches have colonnades along the rear and sides of the building. Because of the mild climate in Greece, the diminutive size of many of the churches, and the informality of worship, many people spend some time outside the building. In any case, on important occasions, there will usually be insufficient room inside for all the worshippers, so that a shady area outside is desirable to accommodate the overflow. *(Right)*

Inside a Greek Church

The interior of a church was anciently divided into three parts: the narthex, nave and chancel, corresponding to three types of worshipper: the catechumens (learners preparing for baptism), the baptised laity, and the clergy. In the *narthex,* or vestibule, in early centuries the catechumens and penitents stood during those parts of the services they were allowed to attend. Today, with the practice of infant baptism almost universal, the catechumens have vanished, and so too, has the narthex. For this reason, churches are now divided into two main parts: the nave, where the laypeople congregate, and the chancel (*bema*), separated from it by the icon screen.

On entering the nave, the visitor will notice that there are no statues, since only two-dimensional images are permitted. However, the entire surface of the interior may be covered by brightly-coloured images: a picture book for the faithful, who in past ages may not have been able to read or write. In the heyday of the Byzantine Empire, magnificent churches would be decorated with mosaics, and less splendid buildings with frescos.

In ancient times mosaics had been used to decorate the floors of rooms and court-yards, but the Byzantines adopted them for the walls of their churches. They discovered how to make the images come alive by setting the tesserae slightly unevenly, so that as the spectator passes, the light catches them, and they seem to flicker and shimmer. In particular, the eyes of the figures seem to follow the observer – an effect which Arnold Toynbee described as "minute in terms of physical measurements but … magical in its effect." [2]

Mosaics from the monastery church of Osios Lukas, Central Greece:
Left: Daniel in the Lion's Den   *Right: The Resurrection*

Today, fresco, the application of paint on plaster, is the normal means of decoration; although many new church buildings may remain with whitewashed, or partly whitewashed, walls for some time, before it is possible to cover them with paintings.

Naturally, the frescos in Greek churches are almost always in Byzantine style. Unfortunately, during the nine-teenth century some painters who worked under Italian influence affected a sentimental Western style. Their work is most frequently encountered in the larger, older, town centre churches, which were mostly built during this uninspired period.

The relative positions of the images placed on the interior wall surfaces is quite strictly determined by tradition; the images being carefully ranked by importance.

Thus over the sanctuary the semi-circular ceiling of the central apse is usually dominated by the *Theotokos*, Mary, the Mother of God. The proportions of the Christ child are always portrayed as those of an adult, rather than a baby, indicating his divine nature from conception.

The central dome always displays the image of Christ *Pantokrator*, "the ruler of all things". There are countless variations on this traditional theme. The halo surrounding the head of Christ usually contains a cross. His robes tend to be depicted in the royal colours: blue and red. On either side of the central figure are the first and last letters of the Greek alphabet, *alpha* and *omega*, signifying that Christ is eternal: "the Alpha and the Omega, the First and the Last, the Beginning and the End."

The Nave

The interior of the church proper is divided into two parts: the nave, where the laypeople congregate, and the chancel (*bema*), separated from it by the icon screen. It is in the nave that the lay worshippers gather to take part in the services.

Just inside the entrance will be found a small icon stand, on which the icon of the patron saint or mystery to which the church is dedicated is usually placed. On important days the icon of the saint or mystery of the day will be displayed there. In small chapels, this may be placed outside the door. Other large icons will usually be displayed in permanent fixed shrines, usually at the rear and down the sides of the nave.

Left : Stand for the icon of the church or of the day inside the nave
Right: Icon placed outside the door of a small chapel..
Below Left: An important icon, diplayed at the front of the nave
Below Centre and Left: Permanent icon icon stands or shrines at the rear and down the sides of the nave.

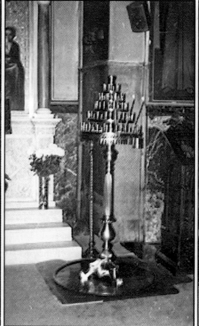

Beside the icon shrines are stands for the burning of votive candles. In small chapels, these are sometimes placed outside the building (centre). In small chapels measures are sometimes taken to prevent damage to the frescos (right).

In large churches a permanent bench may be installed at the back of the church for the sale of candles, books and other items.

After the brightly painted walls, the most striking thing that a visitor may notice inside a Greek church is the lack of pews, those long wooden benches which can sometimes make Western churches seem so cluttered. In a Greek church, seating is usually provided only for the aged and infirm. This consists primarily of fixed benches along the side walls, which are designed for supporting a person who is standing up, by allowing him to lean back against the narrow seat, rather than as conventional seats. There may also be some movable chairs.

The absence of rows of fixed pews allows the creation of a more fluid, informal atmosphere, where people are able to move about freely during the services, and also serves to highlight the essentially collective nature of Orthodox worship.

Long galleries may run the length of the sides and the rear of the nave. These are used for overflow accommodation during particularly well-attended services. The galleries on either side of the nave are usually occupied by women.

Greeks are great lovers of chandeliers, and their churches are no exception. The custom in monasteries, on occasions of special rejoicing, is tospin the chandeliers at important points during the service. This practice has now spread to some parish churches.

In the space in front of the icon screen, steps lead up to a raised platform known as the *solea*. Here the deacon leads the congregation in prayer, and important ceremonies, particularly those which take place during Great Week (Western Holy Week), and rituals such as baptisms, weddings and funerals, are also conducted.

The *solea* may be cordoned off from the rest of the nave by a low barrier, in order to preserve the space necessary for the ceremonial.

On the north side of the *solea*, stands the pulpit (*ambo*), from which the Gospel is read and from which a sermon may be preached. These used to be rare items of furniture in Greek churches, since the practice of preaching was rare; but today they are installed in all parish churches as a matter of course.

On the south side of this space stands the bishop's throne, usually made of wood or marble, raised on three steps and sometimes set under a wooden canopy. At the back of the seat is an image of Christ as the Good Shepherd or the High Priest. This throne, usually empty, is a reminder that the bishop himself is the proper president at the services in all the churches of his diocese, and that the local priests are merely his agents.

On the very far sides of the *solea* stand the desks for the cantors, or chanters. There are usually three seats for the senior cantors on each side, while the others stand around the lectern, or reading desk, which usually revolves so that the books can be made visible to the people on each side, or moved out of the way of the leading singers.

Top left: Pulpit

Top right: Bishop's throne

Top centre: representation of Christ the High Priest on the rear panel of a bishop's chair

Left: The seats for the chanters, and the reading desk in front of it for the service books.

The Icon Screen

Dominating the nave is the *iconostasis* (*templon*): a high carved screen constructed of wood or marble, and covered with icons, which divides the nave from the chancel, and which is pierced by three doorways. For Western visitors, this is perhaps the most conspicuous feature of a Greek church building.

In early centuries, the screen reached only a low height, and was usually made of marble or stone. From the fifth century onwards, the icon screens became higher and more elaborate, and were sometimes made of intricately carved wood, or even ivory. In time they evolved into the complex icon stands we see today, although the lower part of the screen usually remains of stone or marble, perhaps with sculptural or painted decorations.

The *iconostasis*, unknown in Western Churches, is frequently an occasion for criticism, since it is said to isolate the priest and the main action of the services from the people. However, Peter Hammond argues: "It would, I fancy, be generally acknowledged by all who have worshipped among Greek Christians as well as in the churches of the Latins [Roman Catholics] that as an instrument for creating a sense of separation between ministers and people the *iconostasis* of the Easterlings is vastly inferior to the Frankish quire or chancel. An Orthodox priest who has celebrated the liturgy in more than two hundred western churches (most of them Anglican) has remarked that he finds himself far more cut off from his congregation in an English parish church - without an *ikonostasis* of course, but with a long chancel, often having a screen at its *western* end - than in an Orthodox church where the screen is never further away than four feet from the altar."

Guy Mayfield observes that in traditionally placing the altar at the far eastern wall, raised on steps, together with the great length of the traditional chancel, Western architects sought to impress the worshipper with the distance between God and man; while the East does this with the icon screen, obviating the need for physical remoteness.[3]

The icons on the screen are arranged in a particular order. Over the central doorway is usually placed a representation of the Last Supper, and above that, Christ on the Cross with the Virgin and Saint John on each side, as in medieval Western rood screens. On the right of the central door are the icons of Christ and St. John the Baptist, on the left the Virgin Mary and the saints to whom the building is dedicated. Above the principal row of icons are the apostles, or the mysteries of the faith, celebrated in the festivals of the Church.

Oil lamps hang before the iconostasis, as well as before other icons in the church.

The chancel, or *bema*, the part of the church beyond the iconostasis, is divided into three parts: in the centre is the sanctuary, to the north, or left, the *prothesis*, and to the south, or right, the *diaconicon*.

The central entrance to the sanctuary, the "Beautiful Doors" or "Royal Doors" usually display the Annunciation to Mary or an image of Christ as high priest. This doorway is used only by the officiating ministers during the services.

The other two doors are often decorated with icons of the archangels Michael and Gabriel. They are used by cantors, altar boys and other church functionaries. Here the parishioners meet the clergy for various purposes, such as to arrange for baptisms, or to hear confessions.

Beyond the Veil

In the northern section of the chancel, the *prothesis*, stands the credence table, or table of oblation, employed for the preparation of the bread and wine used in the celebration of the Liturgy. The chalice, the cup for the wine used during the liturgy, and the *diskos*, or paten, the round plate on a stand, for the bread, are kept on this table. Here is also placed a special knife, called the spear, which is used for cutting the bread, and a liturgical spoon for administering holy communion. There are also special covers for the chalice and *diskos* and a cruciform piece of metal called the asterisk, or star, which prevents the cloth cover from touching the eucharistic bread underneath. A sponge and cloths for drying the chalice after the liturgy are also kept here.

The southern section of the chancel, the *diakonikon*, is a vestry, where the sacred ministers put on and take off their sacerdotal vestments.

The sanctuary, the middle section of the bema, or chancel, contains the altar. Behind the altar, around the wall of the apse, are seats for priests, with the bishop's throne in the middle.

There is almost always only one altar in a Greek church, and it is usually square: a block of stone containing holy relics consecrated by a bishop. Under normal circumstances it is covered with several cloths. One of these is the *antimension*, a cloth depicting Christ in the tomb, which contains the signature of the bishop, and constitutes his permission for the local community to gather as the Church in that place. The word *antimension* means "instead of the table". Since the bishop is the proper pastor of the Church, the *antimension* stands in for the bishop's own altar, which is in his cathedral. It contains a relic, a tiny part of the body of a saint. This custom originated from the early practice of celebrating the Eucharist on the graves of martyrs who had died for the faith.

Upon the altar is placed a cross, or painted crucifix, the tabernacle, the Gospel book, a service book or missal (*ieratikon*), and two or four candlesticks. The tabernacle or pyx, which often takes the form of a miniature church made of precious metal, is a container for the consecrated bread reserved for the communion of the sick, and the chrism or holy oil. A lighted lamp hangs before it. Underneath the Gospel book is placed the corporal (*eliton*), a silken cloth decorated with an image of the burial of Christ. During the liturgy, this is spread over the centre of the altar, and upon it the sacred vessels containing the bread and wine are placed. Behind the altar may stand the processional cross, a cross fixed on a pole, like a banner. This usually has an image of the crucifixion on one side and the resurrection on the other. On either side of it may stand two silver ceremonial fans, or flabella (*hexapteryga*), having on either face images of six-winged seraphim, which symbolise the presence of the angelic beings in the sanctuary and in the worship of the Church. Behind everything else may be placed the large painted wooden crucifix which is used in the ceremonies of Great (Holy) Week.

The area of the sanctuary is considered a holy place. No one is permitted to enter it unnecessarily, and then only with the blessing of the priest. Lay people, including acolytes or altar servers and parish officials, are not permitted to touch anything on the Holy Table or on the Table of Oblation.

Countryside and Private Chapels

The countryside of Greece is dotted with small chapels of unknown age. Some stand on sites previously occupied by pagan sanctuaries, and incorporate ancient stonework in their fabric.

Ancient temples were frequently built in beautiful places. Thus the later chapels may also be sited in the most striking of locations, such as in the mouths of caves, by the seashore, and on hilltops or cliff-faces.

Very noticeable to visitors to some parts of Greece, particularly the islands of the Aegean, are the very large number of tiny chapels, built privately by individuals as works of piety, often in to fulfil a vow or in thanksgiving for surviving a storm at sea. There are said to be over four hundred on the small island of Mykonos alone.

There is today, however, another, and far less pious, reason why such chapels continue to be erected. It is said that in areas of natural beauty, where building is strictly regulated, it is always easier to obtain a permit to erect a church than to build a house. Those who wish to build themselves a house on a plot of land they own will apply for a permit to erect a chapel, build a tiny one, and then erect a large house beside it; the house itself being "technically" nothing more than a "store" for the chapel.

The description of the architecture and furnishings of a Greek church given above constitutes an ideal which is not reached in all churches, particularly in small countryside and private chapels. Here, there may only be room for one space behind the *iconostasis*, and only one or two doorways piercing the screen. There will also be other modifications to the general plan. A small church or chapel, for example, will usually lack a pulpit and a throne for the bishop, and many have no frescos. Their furnishings may be "homely", or even crude and shabby.

In some venerable churches and chapels, the smoke from the burning of thousands of candles over the centuries has so blackened the walls that not only are the murals effaced by smoke, but to the uninitiated eye the building may appear to be suffering from extensive fire damage.

Many small country chapels, particularly those located in isolated places, are used only once a year, on the day of the festival to which it is dedicated. Others may not be used for public services at all and have become, or always were, simply shrines.

Left: Chapel with burned appearance due to smoke of candle flames
Right: Typical furnishings of small rural chapel

2

Windows onto a Spiritual World

Although three-dimensional images are forbidden throughout the Orthodox Church, it is difficult to overestimate the importance of icons, two-dimensional images painted on wood, in the religious life of the Greeks.

Icons are to be seen everywhere in Greece: in homes, shops, cafes and public buildings, as well as in churches. Their popularity may be seen in the number of shops dedicated almost entirely to the sale of cheap reproductions. In courtrooms, judges sit below an icon of Christ. In every police station an icon of Christ will be displayed. In homes a corner is traditionally designated as a place for the icons, with a lamp or lamps hanging before them. There incense may be burned and prayers offered. People habitually go into the churches during the morning to pray and light candles before the icons.

The icons also play a very important role in Orthodox public worship. They are consecrated before use, decorated with flowers, and honoured by lamps or candles which are placed before them. Some are incensed during public worship, and may be carried in procession on special occasions.

The Painting of Icons

The word "icon" is derived from the Greek word *eikon*, meaning "image". The religious icons of Greece, and of the other Orthodox Churches, are painted according to very strict conventions. This is because the purpose of icons is religious, not decorative. They are neither simple representations of nature nor the products of the individual imagination of the artist.

There is usually no perspective in an icon: the image existing in two-dimensional space.

The golden glow of the icons, signifying the heavenly state of those depicted on them

33

Above left: The Annunciation
   (Byzantine Museum, Athens)

Above right: Christ the Vine
   (Byzantine Museum, Athens)

Right: Panayia "Madre della Consolazione"
   (Byzantine Museum, Athens)

Saint John the Baptist (Byzantine Museum, Athens)

When there is some perspective, it is always in some way odd; there may be several different perspectives in the same picture, or the vanishing point may be in front of the icon rather than behind.

Often the background is entirely of gold. This represents the light of heaven, from which the figures depicted look down upon us. Certain icons which depict those great moments in the story of Christ's incarnation when the divine activity most clearly and dramatically irrupted into the world, for example the Transfiguration, Resurrection and Ascension, often show a circular or almond-shaped blue-white light, known as a mandorla.

The size of the figures depicted is often determined by their importance, rather than by the normal rules of perspective. Bodies are frequently elongated, particularly the hands. This is designed to indicate that the body has already undergone a degree of glorification or spiritualisation. While subordinate figures are shown from the side, the chief figures almost

Worshippers venerating icons

always look directly out of the icon at the viewer.

   Icons are traditionally manufactured in the following manner. First a wooden panel is chosen as a base. This is then covered with several layers of chalk or alabaster powder mixed with gelatine. When this has dried, the panel is sanded smooth. Then the outline of the image to be painted is etched onto it with a sharp awl. The gilded background is then put on. The painting of the figures is achieved with a mixture of water, egg yolk and powdered pigments. The colours are put on in order, from darker to lighter, ending with the flesh pigment for hands and faces. Then lettering which identifies the subject of the icon is added afterwards. Finally, if the icon is not freestanding, a red border is painted around it.

   As the painting of icons is a process which depends upon following an old tradition very closely, they are not free creations of the artists' imagination. For this reason, an icon is never signed by an artist, since his work is held to be an expression of the divinely-inspired tradition, and not the mere product of the individual artist's fantasy.

Especially venerated icons are recognisable by the tamata, or small metal plates attached to the stand by those who wish for some petition to be answered.
The tamata are stamped with a picture indicating the nature of the petition.
Such icons will also be partly covered by silver plate.

The Veneration of Icons

Some exceptional icons have the reputation of working miracles. These may be adorned with votive plaques (*tamata*) depicting ears, eyes, and other parts of the human anatomy by those who have appealed to the saint depicted in the icon for a cure. Today in Athens small plastic dolls are frequently left before icons to represent babies Famous icons are also almost entirely covered with silver-gilt plates, leaving only the faces of the painted figures visible.

Quite a few icons are associated with stories as to their being "found" under mysterious, or even miraculous, circumstances. Perhaps someone saw a light shining on a hillside or in a cave mouth from a distance, and on approaching discovered the icon. It is said that others came from the sea, and were found washed ashore.

One of the most famous icons of the Orthodox world, called *Axion estin,*("It is worthy" lies in the central church of the monastic community of Mount Athos at Karyes. The following story is told about it.

One day in 980 a single monk in a cell some miles away received an unknown visitor, also a monk, who asked to stay the night. At dawn when they were singing mattins, and it came the time to sing the usual hymn to the Mother of God, the unknown monk began to sing an unknown hymn before the icon of the Virgin in a strangely melodious voice. The monk asked his visitor to write down the words of this new composition, and fetched him a slate. The visitor wrote the words on the slate with his finger. The letters were imprinted so deep that it seemed as though the slate must have been made out of soft clay. The visitor told the astounded monk that in future this hymn was to be sung by Orthodox Christians in honour of the Virgin. Then he vanished from his sight.

The astounded monk took the slate to Karyes and showed it to the leaders of the community. They, believing their visitor to have been the archangel Gabriel, sent by God to convey the words of his hymn to Mary to men, brought the icon in procession to the church of Karyes, where it has been kept ever since. On two occasions, it has been taken to Athens in a Greek warship with great ceremony, there to be venerated by the people.

A copy of the mysterious icon of Christ "not made with hands" imprinted upon cloth sent to King Abgar of Edessa, and later preserved in Constantinople. It is believed by many to be the closest we have to a real likeness of the face of Jesus.

Some icons are attributed to the workmanship of Saint Luke the evangelist. To a few others, termed "not made with hands," a supernatural origin has been attributed. The most famous of these is the image of the face of Christ imprinted upon a cloth said to have been sent to King Abgar of Edessa, in Asia, and later taken to Constantinople.

According to the story, King Abgar became a leper. Having heard of Jesus' miracles, he sent his archivist, Ananias, with a letter requesting Christ go to Edessa and heal him. Ananias was painter, and Abgar instructed him to make a portrait of the Saviour if he refused to visit him. Ananias made a portrait, but because Christ was surrounded by a great crowd, and because his face kept changing, and could not be captured by the artist, Ananias was unable to finish the job.

Seeing his difficulty, Jesus asked for some water, and wiped his face with a linen towel. His features were imprinted on this cloth, which he gave to Ananias. When he received the miraculous portrait, Abgar was partially healed. After the Ascension, Thaddeus went to Edessa, completely the process of healing the king and converted him. The holy image was placed above the gate of the town and Abgar spent the rest of his reign spreading Christianity throughout his kingdom. Later the bishop of the town had it bricked up into its niche, and placing a lamp before it. Time passed, and the place was forgotten, but it was rediscovered when Cosroes, king of the Persians, besieged the city in 544 or 545. The lamp was still burning. Not only was the image intact, but it had also been imprinted on the inner side of the tile which had concealed it from view.

The Theology of Icons

Such popular stories as that of the Mandylion might suggest that the veneration of icons is entirely a matter of popular superstition. But icons have a very important place in Orthodox theology, where they are not thought of as simple pictures or as representations, but are seen as an integral part of God's revelation of Himself to mankind, and as windows onto the spiritual world. They are regarded as the visible representations of the invisible

Queue of worshippers waiting outside the cathedral of Athens

presence they represent: "... the purpose of the icon is not to remind the faithful of those who are absent, but to make the invisible world visible to the eye of faith."

In answer to the charge of idolatry, frequently raised by Protestants and others, the Orthodox, like the Catholics, distinguish between *worship* and *veneration*. The Orthodox say that they do not worship icons; they revere, or venerate, them. That is, they accord to them a profound honour; but this falls far short of offering to them the worship which is due to God alone. Moreover, the homage or veneration offered before an icon is, strictly speaking, offered not to the object itself, but to the one(s) whom it portrays.

This veneration is soundly based upon the theology of the Incarnation. Saint John of Damascus pointed out that "Since the Invisible One became visible by taking flesh, you can fashion the image of Him whom you saw." By becoming man, the Invisible made Himself visible, the Infinite made himself finite. It is this visible and finite manifestation of God in Christ which the icon painter captures, and which the worshipper uses as a means to direct his own bodily and limited attention towards the Invisible and Infinite.

Moreover, the veneration of icons is held to safeguard the attitude of the worshipper towards the material world in a very important way. There is always a tendency among religious people to denigrate and downvalue the material world. This may manifest itself in puritanism or, in extreme form, in an outright dualism which regards everything material as intrinsically evil. In the Christian faith, however, the world is the creation of a supremely good and all-powerful God; and in the Incarnation this God took upon himself human flesh and a fully human personality, in order that humanity, and with it matter, might be redeemed and glorified, fulfilling properly the end which God intended for them. Thus the special nature of the icon as a channel of divine grace is itself a symbol of all the inherent spiritual potentiality of matter.

3

Heaven on Earth

There are several features which distinguish Orthodox worship from what is customary among Catholics and Protestants.

Men and women usually stand on different sides of the church: men on the south (the right looking towards the altar), and the women on the north (or left). Sometimes there is a gallery along the back and sides of the church for the women. The separation of the sexes is breaking down in urban areas, and particularly at the back of the church, where people will stand together without discrimination.

Unlike the churches of Northern Europe and North America, the worshippers attending a religious service are not all constrained to arrive or depart at the same time. A foreign visitor may recognise an important part of a service by the visible swelling, and subsequent diminution of numbers in the congregation as people come and go. During the services the worshippers are not regimented to adopt the same bodily postures, nor are they constrained to remain rooted to one spot for the entire period.

The usual posture of worship in the Eastern Church is standing. Kneeling is rarely prescribed, and during Eastertide it is entirely forbidden. Under special circumstances, such as on approaching a pilgrimage shrine, worshippers may sometimes prostrate themselves. Increasingly, sitting down for parts of the long services is becoming more and more acceptable, leading to an increase in the number of seats placed in the naves of the churches.

Since the buildings are oriented, the worshipper normally faces east. However, if there is something important happening during the course of a service, such as the passing of a procession, the people will naturally turn towards it.

The congregation rarely takes an audible part in the services; they mostly participate by repeatedly crossing themselves at certain points, and by venerating particular icons by lighting candles or praying before them.

The language used in the church is that of the New Testament, pronounced in the manner of contemporary Greek. This is generally comprehensible to Greeks who have learned *katharevousa*, the purified form of the language, which was taught to all school-children until the 1970s, but only to some high school students since that date. As a result, elderly and middle-aged people are often quite at home with the language, while an it is an increasing problem that younger people may not understand it. However, those who have been reared upon it from an early age without any schooling in the language usually feel quite at home with it, in the same way that most native English-speaking opera lovers cannot

Worshippers lighting votive candles

follow word for word the Italian or the German librettos of the operas they love, but that makes little difference to their ability to appreciate the performance. The Orthodox Churches in general are happy to have the liturgy celebrated in any language understood by the majority of the worshippers, but the Greek Church is understandably reluctant to jettison a language which uniquely connects it to the Gospel, to the Apostolic Age, and to the very origins of the Church.

Incense, which symbolises the rising of the prayers of the people to God, is an invariable accompaniment of public worship. The thuribles used for this purpose in church have bells attached to them. It is a common practice for lay people to burn incense before their own icons at home, particularly on important days.

Music

All formal religious services are sung, and there are no "said" services; but no musical instruments whatsoever are used.

The visitor should be warned that the music of the Greek Church cannot be instantly appreciated by Westerners. Unlike the music of, say, the Russian or Rumanian Churches, which is readily acceptable at first hearing, the sounds of the Greek chant are markedly unfamiliar to the Western ear, and initially they may be perceived as discordant. This is because, like much eastern music, the early style developed in Constantinople, which is still used in the Greek Church, employs notes on the scale which lie *between* the familiar notes of the modern piano. Byzantine music has inherited micro-tonal intervals from the music of ancient Greece and the Jewish Synagogue. For this reason, Byzantine music is able to produce melodies that could not possibly be played using the more familiar European scales.

Another factor affecting appreciation is that it was originally composed, and for centuries used, in a society where the sense of time was profoundly different from our own. In order to appreciate it, the visitor will need to forget that he has a wristwatch, and relax for some length of time.

Liturgical Poetry

With the toleration of Christianity in 330, for the first time, Christians could worship as they chose. This soon led to a great increase of music in worship. But it was during the reign of Justinian that a degree of splendour was added to every aspect of religious life. Increasing numbers of hymns were produced to enrich the liturgical services of the church. Gradually, music and hymnography took a major role in the liturgy, and the singing and chanting became increasingly popular. Several distinctive forms of Byzantine hymnography, such as the *kontakion* and the litany emerged.

The *kontakion* is a hymn based upon the mystery or saint commemorated on a particular day. Some, in translation, have been familiar to Western congregations as hymns since the nineteenth century.

The litany (*ektine*) occurs frequently in Orthodox worship. These are lists of petitions addressed to God by the deacon. He stands before the royal doors holding the end of his stole in his right hand, and at the end of each petition, he crosses himself with it and bows. The cantors respond "Lord have mercy" to each petition. Meanwhile the priest prays silently, and when the petitions are ended, he reads the end of his prayer aloud.

By the eleventh and twelfth centuries there were so many hymns already in use in the church that hymnography was for a time outlawed.

To Western taste, the words of the Orthodox services tend to be appear elaborate and repetitive, lacking the brevity of, for example, Roman Catholic services. This is because rhythmical compositions make up perhaps some eighty per cent of the contents of the Greek service books. They are, however, frequently of great poetic merit.

The Office

There are two types of divine service, the Liturgy and the regular round of daily worship based upon the Psalms, developed for the use of the monks.

The daily office is based, as in the Roman Catholic Church, upon the recitation of the psalms and readings from the scriptures. The offices of the Greek Church correspond roughly to those of the Roman Catholics, namely: vespers, compline, lauds, matins, prime, terce, sext and none. However, they are much more variable with the seasons of the year than are the rather simple and schematic Western services. They also contain much more religious poetry. There are also many long prayers to be recited silently by the priest while the choir sings the psalms. The Psalter is divided into twenty parts, each of which is made up of three sections, and the whole is sung every week.

The full office lasts sung in choir lasts about eight hours, but this is confined to monasteries. Offices are sometimes recited in parish churches on the day before a special holy day, when vespers matins and prime may be sung in the evening.

At Vespers every day is sung the famous hymn *phos ilaron*, as the evening light disappears, and the lamps are lit. It has been translated into many languages and is used as a hymn by Christians of many denominations:

"Hail, gladdening Light, poured from his pure glory
Who is the immortal Father, heavenly, blest,
Holiest of Holies, Jesus Christ, our Lord.
Now we are come to the sun's hour of rest,
The lights of evening shine around us,
We hymn the divine Father, Son and Holy Spirit:
Worthiest are You at all times to be praised
With undefiled tongue,
Son of God, akone giver of life.
Therefore throughout all the world, Lord, they acknowledge Your glory."

The Liturgy

Arnold Toynbee observes: "For Eastern Orthodox Christians, the heart of religion is not theology; it is the liturgy."[1] The Orthodox would claim that the Church can only be understood through its Liturgy, which expresses visibly the life of the Church, uniting in worship the Church in heaven and on earth.

The Liturgy proper is the service which corresponds to the Mass in the Roman Catholic Church and the Holy Eucharist or Communion in Protestant Churches. It arose out of the Last Supper, when Jesus took bread, blessed it and gave it to his disciples saying "Take, eat, this is my body"; and took wine, blessed it, and gave it to them saying "This is my blood." After his resurrection, the early Christians did that regularly in his memory from the very beginning. In a very short time, it developed into the central act of Christian worship, with the addition, immediately before it, of a service of scripture readings and prayer.

For the Orthodox, the Liturgy is the centre of the Christian life, the meeting place of the divine and human, when the God-man Christ becomes bread and wine, and his Church on earth participates in His self-offering for the redemption of mankind. The Orthodox see the Liturgy both as a re-enactment of the Incarnation and as participation in this world in the worship of the angels in heaven. As such, they seek to perform the Liturgy with an appropriate solemnity and magnificence.

When the emissaries of Prince Vladimir of Kiev arrived at Constantinople in search of a faith for his realm, they attended the Liturgy in the magnificent church of Ayia Sophia. On their return they reported: We did not know whether we were in heaven or on earth, for assuredly on earth such beauty cannot be found anywhere else, So we do not know what we ought to tell you; but one thing we know well: God dwells among those who celebrate His glory in such a manner that no other religion on this earth could equal. It is impossible for us to forget such splendorous beauty ."[2]

There are three different orders of service. The oldest, called the liturgy of St. Basil, is now used only on the Sundays of Lent (except on Palm Sunday), Great Thursday, and Great Saturday, the vigils of Christmas and the Epiphany, and on St. Basil's Day (January 1st). On most other days the liturgy of St. John Chrysostom, which is really just a shortened form of that of St. Basil, is used. On the weekdays of Lent (except Saturdays) no liturgy proper is be said. On these days, the Liturgy of the Presanctified, attributed to St. Gregory, is employed instead. On these occasions, there is no actual consecration of the bread and wine.

The Orthodox do not celebrate the liturgy every day, usually only on Sundays and greater feast-days. Moreover, the liturgy is never celebrated more than once on the same day at the same altar. It is rarely celebrated more than once on the same day in the same church, since where it is there must be two altars, which is itself a rare occurrence. Similarly, a priest never celebrates twice on the same day. Where many priests are present, they all *con*celebrate, or celebrate together. This means that the Liturgy has retained its congregational character. Thus there is no parallel in Orthodoxy to the Roman Catholic celebration of "private masses". Moreover, as all celebrations of the liturgy are accompanied by singing and incense, there is no such thing as a "low mass" either.

The liturgy was originally formed of two parts, a service of scripture reading and the communion service. Only baptised and confirmed believers could attend both. Those who were not baptised, but in preparation for initiation into the Christian Church, and known as catechumens, were allowed to remain for the first part only. Thus the first part was known as the Liturgy of the Catechumens, and the second as the Liturgy of the Faithful. In time, a third ritual of preparation was added at the beginning, giving us the three-fold form which is found everywhere today.

The Rite of Preparation

The priest and deacon begin by making three reverences towards the *iconostasis*, and then say some preparatory prayers. When they have kissed the icons, they enter the door to the *diakonikon and* put on their vestments, the priest first blessing each one, and saying special prayers.

The elaborate changes of colours of the vestments of the sacred ministers used in the Catholic Church – white at Easter, red at Pentecost, purple during Advent and Lent, green on other occasions, etc. – never developed in the East. The principle of choice is simply that the richer and more magnificent vestments are worn on the greater occasions,

Top: paten, with asterisk, lance and spoon
Above: Thuribles for burning incense
Below: Liturgical fan, representing the presence of the angels

regardless of colour. However, there is a tendency to use black or purple in preference to others on Great Friday.

Having vested, the sacred ministers wash their hands and go across to the *prothesis*, credence table, or table of oblation, where the deacon has already placed the sacred vessels, and the bread and wine.

The chief vessels are the chalice, the cup for the wine, and the *diskos*, or paten, the round plate on a stand, for the bread. The star, or asterisk, consists of two arched metal bands held together by a screw in the shape of a cross. It is placed over the paten to prevent the veil which covers them from touching the bread underneath. The lance, a small, double-edged knife, is used to cut the bread. A spoon is required to administer communion, and a sponge to cleanse the sacred vessels after use. There is a veil each for the paten and chalice, and a third and larger one, the *aer*, to cover both .

A round loaf of leavened bread is marked with divisions, the parts to be consecrated have a cross between the letters "IC. XC. NI. KA" (an abbreviation of "Jesus Christ conquers"). The priest takes the holy lance, cuts away this part, while the deacon pours wine and water into the chalice. The priest then cuts away a particle from the rest of the bread in honour of the Mother of God, and nine others for various Saints, and others for the bishop, clergy and people for whom he wishes to pray. These particles are placed on the *diskos*. Both the *diskos* and the chalice, covered with their veils, and are incensed. The deacon then incenses the *prothesis*, altar, sanctuary, nave, and priest. They both go to the altar, kiss the book of Gospels on it, and the deacon, says, "It is time to do sacrifice to the Lord!" The doors of the *iconostasis* are opened, and the deacon enters the nave.

The Liturgy of the Catechumens
The second part of the liturgy opens with an act of adoration, "Blessed is the King-dom of the Father, and of the Son, and of the Holy Spirit, now and for ever, world without end," followed by a litany recited by the deacon. This series of petitions is continually broken by the response *Kyrie eleison* (Lord have mercy) sung by the cantors. It opens with the petition "For the peace that is from above and for the salvation of our souls, let us pray to the Lord," continuing with intercessions for clergy and people, for the peace of the world and the unity of the Church, for earthly rulers, for the fruits of the earth, for travellers, for the sick and suffering and for those in prison. It is followed by the anthems, ending with the Beatitudes from the Sermon on the Mount, sung by the choir.

There follows the "Little Entrance" a symbolic representation of the coming of Christ to earth. The priest takes the book of the Gospels from the altar and hands it to the deacon. Preceded by candle-bearers and censers in procession, they pass together through the north door into the nave through the congregation. In the middle of the nave, the deacon raises the book above his head and cries "Wisdom! Stand upright!" They return to the altar through the royal door, while the choir sings the anthem "O come, let us worship and bow down to Christ."

The choir then sings the *Trisagion*: "Holy God, Holy Mighty, Holy Immortal, have mercy upon us," which derives its name from the threefold repetition of the word "holy". This is followed by a reading from one of the epistles in the New Testament, usually by one

45

of the cantors. With the singing of "Alleluia", the deacon takes the book of the Gospels to the *ambo* or pulpit, and reads the Gospel for the day. The book is then handed to the priest who carries it back to the altar and the doors are closed. Meanwhile the deacon takes up his position before the *iconostasis*, and recites a litany for all sorts and conditions of men. At this point in the early church, the catechumens were required to leave the building, and even today, the deacon says "Let the catechumens depart. Let all the catechumens depart. Let no catechumens remain."

The Liturgy of the Faithful

The Liturgy of the faithful begins with a further litany recited by the deacon, while the priest at the altar silently recites prayers in preparation for the coming sacrifice. This is followed by the Great Entrance, perhaps visually the most dramatic part of the service, which symbolizes the entry of Christ into Jerusalem to meet his Passion and Death. The priest covers the deacon's shoulders with the *aer* (the great veil), and gives him the diskos with the bread, covered with its own smaller veil. The deacon holds the diskos as high as his head, the thurible hanging from one of his fingers. The priest follows with the chalice filled with wine and water covered with its own veil. Acolytes, candle-bearers and fan-bearers, go in front in solemn procession. They pass through the north door while the worshippers bow their heads and repeatedly make the sign of the Cross. As they return through the royal door, the choir sings the Cherubic Hymn: "Let us, who mystically represent the Cherubim and who sing to the life-giving Trinity the thrice-holy hymn, put away all earthly cares so as to receive the King of all things escorted by the army of angels. Alleluia, alleluia, alleluia." At the altar the priest puts down the chalice, takes the diskos from the deacon, puts it down and incenses the offering again. The priest and deacon say some more prayers for each other and that God may accept their sacrifice, and then the deacon cries out: "The doors, the doors. Let us attend in wisdom" and the Nicene Creed is read.

At this point there begins the *Anaphora or* Canon of the Mass, the great prayer of thanksgiving and consecration. The priest blesses the people and then sings "Lift up your hearts." The choir respond "We have them with the Lord." The priest sings "Let us give thanks to the Lord." The singers respond: "It is meet and just to adore the Father, Son, and Holy Spirit, one consubstantial and undivided Trinity." The priest then continues: "It is meet and just to sing to You, to bless You, praise You, and give thanks to You in all places. ..." And so the Eucharistic prayer continues. This first part is said silently by the priest, who raises his voice at the words: "... crying, singing, proclaiming the hymn of victory and saying:" and the singers chant: "Holy, holy, holy,". The prayer proceeds to the Words of Institution, used by Christ at the Last Supper, which are read aloud, although the connecting links supplied by the evangelist are recited in a lower tone. The *anamnesis,* or commemoration recalls the Passion and Death of Christ, the Resurrection, the Ascension and looks forward to the Second Coming in glory. The *epiklesis* then invokes the Holy Spirit "upon us and upon these gifts set before You. And make this bread the precious Body of Your Christ and that which is in this cup the precious Blood of Your Christ, changing them by Your Holy Spirit." The priest then passes to intercession, in company with the Virgin Mary and all the saints, for the dead, for the Church and its hierarchy, for rulers and all mankind.

After another litany there follows the "Our Father". The doors are opened, the deacon says, "Let us attend." Then the priest elevates the *diskos* and chalice, saying, "Holy things to the holy people"; and the choir responds: "One only is holy, one only Lord, Jesus Christ in the glory of the Father. Amen." The doors are again closed. The priest breaks the consecrated bread and says, "The Lamb of God is broken and distributed." He then puts the fractions marked IE. into the chalice and the deacon pours in a little warm water. The priest comes to the communion and says: "Behold I come to Christ, our immortal King and God," takes a part marked XC and says: "The precious and most holy Body of Jesus Christ, Lord and God and Saviour, is given to me, N., priest, for the forgiveness of my sins, and for life everlasting," and takes Holy Communion. He then gives communion in the form of bread to the deacon, and the same ceremony with similar words is used for the chalice.

The doors are opened, the deacon shows the people the chalice, and says: "Approach with fear of God, faith and love." The priest goes down to the royal doors and distributes Holy Communion to the people, who receive both bread and wine. The priest takes with a spoon part of the consecrated bread which is in the chalice, and soaked in the consecrated wine, and gives it to the communicant, saying: "The servant of God, N., receives the holy and precious Body and Blood of Jesus Christ, Lord, God, and Saviour, for the forgiveness of his sins, and for life everlasting." The communicant wipes his lips with a silken napkin held over the arm of the deacon, and returns to the body of the church. When he goes back to the altar, the deacon carries the sacred vessels back to the *prothesis*.

There follows the last part of the service, the *Dismissal*. The deacon chants a short litany with the singers, and the priest says a prayer before the image of Christ on the *iconostasis*. The deacon goes to the *prothesis* and consumes all that is left of the Holy Eucharist (with the *prosphora*) and cleanses the sacred vessels.

The bread which was left aside when the offerings were first prepared, and has stayed on the *prothesis* ever since, is brought to the priest, blessed, and distributed to the people as a symbol of fellowship. After a few more prayers, the priest and deacon go to the *diakonikon*, the doors are again shut, and they take off their vestments. They make a short thanksgiving, and the liturgy is over. The entire ceremony takes about two hours.

Private Prayer

In the Orthodox Church, private prayer is seen as an extension into private life of the public prayer of the community, as expressed in the liturgy. For this reason, people may recite liturgical prayers. Perhaps the most commonly used is the *Trisagion*: "Holy God, holy Mighty, holy Immortal One, have mercy upon us (*three times*). Glory to the Father, and to the Son, and to the Holy Spirit; Now and for ever, and from age to age. Amen. Holy God, holy Mighty, holy Immortal One, have mercy upon us."

Those inclined to more strenuous and sustained communion with God, especially the monks, favour the use of the Jesus Prayer. This involves repetition of the name of Jesus, using some form of the formula "Lord Jesus Christ, son of God, have mercy on me, a sinner." It is sometimes associated with certain bodily postures and breathing exercises as a form of meditation. This is described in the *Philokalia*, a collection of writings of mystics dating from a period of over a thousand years.

47

4

The Holy Mysteries

The "holy mysteries" of the Orthodox Church correspond roughly to what Western Christians call sacraments, although the Greek term *mysterion* is rather wider. Sacraments are sacred rites through which, it is believed, the Grace of God is imparted to the faithful by means of some outward physical sign. Orthodox teaching tends to emphasize their mysterious character, by contrast with the more legalistic approach adopted by the Roman Catholic Church. Since the concept in the Orthodox Church is not sharply defined, no precise number of sacraments has been definitively laid down. St. John of Damascus recognized two sacraments only, Baptism (with Chrismation or Confirmation), and the Eucharist. During the mediaeval period a wide variety of sacred rites were considered as sacraments, many being what Roman Catholics would call "sacramentals", but after the Council of Lyons of 1274 the Western usage of seven sacraments (Baptism, Confirmation, Penance, the Eucharist, Ordination, Holy Matrimony and Extreme Unction) was frequently adopted. The traditional attitude of the Orthodox Church, however, is to consider every act of the Church as intrinsically sacramental.

Baptism and Confirmation

The sacraments of Baptism and Confirmation are the rites of Christian initiation, the means whereby a person is made a member of the Church.

In the early Church, the candidates for initiation were adult converts. They underwent a period of instruction and preparation, during which they were called catechumens, before being baptised, usually at Easter. Later, baptisms were held any time of the year, and in an increasingly Christian world, infant

An ancient baptismal font, Rhodes town.

48

*The rite of exorcism
at the door of the church
before baptism*

baptism became the norm. In the Western Church, two parts of the process of initiation, rebirth during immersion in water (Baptism) and receiving the gift of the Holy Spirit (Confirmation or Chrismation) were separated, baptism being administered soon after birth, and confirmation during late childhood or adolescence. In the Orthodox Church, Baptism and Confirmation both take place at the same ceremony, so that an infant is fully admitted to the company of the faithful and made a full member of the Church on a single occasion.

The logic of the ritual requires that the candidate for baptism renounce Satan and accept the Christian faith. As in other Christian Churches in the case of infants this is done by sponsors or godparents. Today in Greece children are usually baptised during the spring or summer months, when they are between six months and one year of age.

Baptism is believed to effect the spiritual rebirth of the recipient. It is the Christian's personal participation in the Resurrection of Christ by anticipation. Owing to the numerous rites which accompany it, many of which go back to the earliest centuries of the Christian faith, the baptismal ritual is quite complicated, although in essence it requires only the three-fold name of God and total immersion in water, except in emergencies.

Since baptism is a rebirth, the immersion into, and emergence from, water is held by the Orthodox to be essential to the symbolism of the rite. Consequently, in the Greek Church, baptism is by total immersion rather than, as in the Western Churches, by merely "wetting the baby's head". However, as in the Western churches, in case of emergency Baptism may be performed by a lay person, and immersion may be replaced by sprinkling.

The first ceremony of the ritual is that of exorcism. The child, held by its godparents, is met by the priest just inside the door of the church. The priest breathes three times on the candidate, on the mouth, breast and forehead, signs him with the sign of the Cross, and reads the ritual of exorcism: "Satan, the Lord exorcizes thee, get thee hence!" Then follows the renunciation, when one of the godparents, on behalf of the candidate, turns to the West, three times, exclaims "I renounce you," and spits in token of his aversion to the Devil. Then turning to the east, he confesses Christ and says three times, "I surrender myself to Christ." One of the godparents then recites the Nicene Creed on behalf of the child being baptised.

The focus of attention then moves from the door of the church to the font. In the Greek church, baptismal fonts are not usually the fixed and elaborately decorated furnishings they

Above: Left: The font prepared for a baptism, and the tablebehind it with everything necessary for the baptism. Centre and right: The blessing of the baptismal waters. Below: Left: the baptism Centre: the baptismal candle Right: The chrism

are in the West. Baptisms are performed in portable metal vats set in the nave of the church before the *solea* for that purpose.

The water is first blessed by the priest, who makes the sign of the cross over it with the book of the Gospels, touches it with the flat of his hand, and breathing upon it.

After anointing of the candidate with holy oil, the priest moves on to the baptism proper. This consists of three immersions accompanied by the formula "The servant of God *N* is baptized in the name of the Father and of the Son and of the Holy Spirit." Through the act of immersion, it is believed that the baptized person dies to this world and is born again in the resurrection of Christ into eternal life.

The child is then clothed with a white baptismal robe to symbolise his new state, and carried, in procession around the baptismal font three times as the symbol of his progression into the Kingdom of God.

There follows immediately the sacrament of Chrismation (or Confirmation), also called

Left: The Chrismation (confirmation)
Right: the new white bapstismal clothes

"anointing" or "sealing". In this sacrament the baptised person is said to receive the gift of the Holy Spirit. The anointing represents the conferring of the gifts of the Holy Spirit to strengthen the candidate for the spiritual life. It is the Christian's personal participation in Pentecost. Those who have been confirmed are full members of the Orthodox Church and may be admitted to the other sacraments. Chrismation is performed by anointing the baptised person with the sign of the cross on the forehead, both eyes, nostrils, mouth and ears.

This ceremony, called in the West "confirmation", is usually performed by the bishop himself. In the East it is performed by a priest, using oil consecrated by the bishops. This oil, also called myrrh (*miron*) is prepared by the bishops on Great Thursday, and is employed to show that the gift of the Spirit was originally given to men through the apostles, whose successors the bishops are.

The ritual is concluded with a tonsure, when the priest cuts the baptismal candidate's hair crosswise. After the reading of the Gospel, the child is given a final blessing at the royal doors.

In addition to the complexity of the religious ritual itself, there has grown up a considerable body of social expectations concerning "how things should be done," and a small industry dedicated to supplying "baptismal goods": special white clothes for the child, specially wrapped sweets for the guests at the church, the baptismal candle, - not to mention the cost of the priest, the cantor, and the inevitable eating and drinking which must follow. As a result, the baptism of a child in Greece has become for many a significant burden, in that it requires a considerable outlay of expense, which it would be socially unacceptable to avoid - rather like weddings in the West.

Approximately forty days after baptism and chrismation, it is customary for the newly-baptised to make a first communion at the normal Sunday liturgy. This is also true of infants. At that time the child is usually taken to church by his or her godparents, who hold the lighted candle which was used at the baptism.

Blessings

There are many occasions when Greeks seek the blessing of a priest, which may be given merely verbally, or more usually with incense, a cross and the sprinkling of holy water, using a sprig of basil. It is customary for the priests to visit, as far as is possible, every home in the country and bless it with holy water on January 5th. Blessings are particularly sought for the initiation of enterprises of any kind. On the first day of the new school year, all teachers and pupils will receive a collective blessing at their school before the first lessons of the new year begin. Parliament opens its annual sessions with a blessing, as does the Thessaloniki Trade Fair. The laying of the foundations of a new building, the launching of a new boat, or the setting up of a new business may each be solemnly sanctified. Individuals also offer everything from icons to motor vehicles to be blessed. The rituals for these are to be found in the *Euchologion*.

Among the blessings rarely omitted are those of a woman and her newly born child forty days after its birth. A woman who had given birth was traditionally regarded as "unclean" for forty days afterwards, and would not be expected to attend any public functions or pay any social calls. However, she was also exempted from the obligation to work in the fields during this period. When, on the fortieth day, she had been to church with

The customary blessing of teachers and pupils at the beginning of the school year

The blessing of a new shop, using incense, cross and holy water

Perhaps the most lengthy and complex of the rituals of blessing is that which is given to a new church building.

The consecration of a church, which must be performed by a bishop, involves the anointing of the walls of the church in twelve places. The heart of the ritual is the consecration of the altar, in which holy relics are deposited.

Right: Anointing the walls of a church using a sponge on the end of a pole during the rite of consecration

Below: The consecration of an altar

her child to be blessed by the priest, her confinement would be ended, and she would be able to resume her normal place in society. Although the concept of "confinement" no longer has its traditional hold over the public mind, the practice of "churching" remains.

The custom of presenting the newly-born child in the church recalls the Old Testament practice of offering male children in the Jerusalem temple, particularly the offering of Christ on the fortieth day after his birth. In the Greek Church both male and female children are formally presented to God in the Church with special prayers. A male child is taken from his mother through the royal doors by the priest and blessed inside the sanctuary. A girl child is blessed in front of the doors, although today some of the more liberal priests are said to take baby girls into the sanctuary as well.

Confession

When a child is old enough to discern right from wrong, he may go to confession. Only grave sins, including prolonged absence from Holy Communion necessitate sacramental penance, although Christians are expected to make use of this sacrament periodically in order deliberately to humble themselves before God and to receive guidance in the Christian life from their pastor.

In the early church, confession was performed publicly before all the congregation, but in recent times it is usually done only in the presence of the priest. Confessions are heard in the nave of the church. There are only very rarely confessional boxes as in Roman Catholic churches, and when there are, they have open glass fronts, and there is no grill between the priest and his penitents. Usually, the penitent stands before the priest and makes his confession with bowed head, upon which the priest places his stole.

The sacrament of has three main elements. The first is a sincere sorrow for sin, and for the breaking of communion with God. The second is an open and sincere confession of sins. The third is the formal prayer of absolution through which the forgiveness of God through Christ is bestowed upon the repentant sinner.

The priest is directed to say " Brother, be not ashamed that you come before God and before me, for you do not confess to me but to God who is present here." He asks the penitent his sins, says that only God can forgive him, but that Christ gave this power to his Apostles, and absolves him with a prayer in which occur the words: "May this same God, through me a sinner, forgive you all now and for ever."

The priest may impose the obligation to say certain prayers, or fasting or a pilgrimage as acts of penance. These are, however, never regarded as acts of satisfaction, or "paying for the sins", but only as a form of discipline. The system of indulgences, which developed during the Middle Ages in the Roman Catholic Church, never established itself among Orthodox Christians.

The Eucharist

The sacrament of the Eucharist is known by many names, such as "the holy Sacrifice", "The Lord's Supper", or "Holy Communion". The service of the Eucharist is known as the liturgy (see Chapter 3 above). It is lies at the heart of the Church's life. The term *Eucharist* is given to the consecrated bread and wine, and to the whole act of gathering, praying, reading the Scriptures remembering Christ's Passion, Death and Resurrection, and eating and drinking his Body and Blood in communion.

Communion is given to all members of the Church, including infants who are baptized and confirmed, and it is always given in both forms bread and wine. The Roman Catholic practice of communion with bread only is regarded as disobedient to Christ's expressed will, and a departure from the common tradition of the Universal Church. An exception to this rule is only made in the case of the smallest children. Leavened bread is used in the Orthodox Liturgy in contrast to the Western use of unleavened wafers. This difference of custom became one of the main points of controversy with the Roman Catholic Church.

The bread must be prepared from pure wheat flour, water, salt, and yeast, using no other ingredients, and carefully prepared. The wine has to be sweet, and made from red grapes, without additives or fortification.

The Orthodox receive holy communion in a state of total fasting. They do so, however, rarely; usually twice a year, at Christmas and Easter. A woman who is having her period may not enter the church building at that time, much less receive holy communion. The sick receive holy communion under both kinds, using bread which has been dipped into the chalice and allowed to dry. It is administered with a spoon.

A distinctive feature of the Orthodox Liturgy is the Invocation or *epiklesis* of the Holy Spirit. After the recital of the Words of Institution in the Great Prayer, God is asked to send down His Holy Spirit, and to transform the bread and wine into the Body and Blood of Christ. While in the West from me fourth century onwards the Words of Institution were invested with consecratory powers, the Eastern Church maintained that no change in the elements took place until after the *epiklesis*.

The Orthodox Church does not agree with the Protestant doctrine that the Body and the Blood of the Eucharist are merely symbols of Christ's Body and Blood, or that the Eucharist a simple memorial meal of Christ's last supper. The Eucharist in the Orthodox Church is understood to be the genuine Body and Blood of Christ. Various ways were developed in the West to try to explain how the bread and the wine become the Body and Blood of Christ in the eucharistic liturgy, particularly in connection with Catholic/Protestant controversies of the sixteenth century. For the Orthodox, these explanations are too rationalistic, and too closely connected with one particular philosophical system. The mystery of the holy Eucharist is said to lie beyond precise human analysis or explanation.

The Eucharist is closely associated in the Orthodox understanding with the doctrine of the Incarnation, and the transformation of the sacramental elements has been described as having a close analogy to the Incarnation. However, "The Roman Church is always trying to define the manner of change in the sacraments; the Eastern Church says it is a mystery."[1] Nevertheless, a favourite way of referring to the change which occurs in the bread and wine as the effect of their consecration is "transformation".

The elements retain their sacred character after the conclusion of the Liturgy, and are reserved and used for the communion of the sick. They are never exposed on the altar for the adoration of the people, as sometimes happens in the Roman Catholic Church. To a Western Christian, the attitude of the Orthodox in general to the sacrament is in some ways difficult to understand. Believing that the bread and wine become in a real sense the body and blood of Christ, the consecrated elements are afforded little especial reverence, certainly as compared with icons. Yet the *un*consecrated bread and wine, processed through the Church at the Greater Entrance during the Liturgy, which the Church teaches are not transformed into the Body and Blood of Christ until the much later invocation of the Holy Spirit, are accorded considerable reverence. Perhaps the answer lies in the much greater consciousness of the Orthodox that the common life of the Church as a whole is the arena of divine grace, leading to a less pronounced tendency to single out the consecrated host as marking the unique presence of God in the world.

Marriage

For many centuries there was no distinctive Christian ritual for marriage at all. When a special ritual was developed, it was patterned after the sacraments of baptism and chrismation.

While the Western Churches (Catholic and Protestant) tend to regard marriage as constituted by the contract between the two partners, followed by physical consummation, the Orthodox Church assigns this role to the service in Church. The Orthodox sacrament of marriage is not a juridical contract, and it contains no vows or oaths. It is rather understood as the "baptizing and confirming" of a human love in God.

There are a number of days when it is forbidden to get married, including throughout the fasting period of Lent, the forty days prior to Easter, that of Advent, the forty days prior to Christmas, and the first fifteen days of August before the feast of the Panayia (August 15th). It is also usually considered that any marriage during a Leap Year is likely to be unlucky.

The couple to be married do not see one another on the day, but the groom asks the bride's father for his daughter's hand in marriage. The groom's best man or *koumbaros*, along with the priest, is in charge of the ceremony. The groom arrives before the bride, and the two families sit on opposite sides of the church. The bride arrives with her father, or a male relative, while the groom travels to the church with his best man.

The wedding service is made up of two formerly separate ceremonies, those of betrothal and marriage proper. They are usually held in the *solea*, the space before the icon screen, around a small table.

The central part of the betrothal service is the blessing and exchange of rings in token of the free consent of both parties to the union. The exchange of rings symbolizes the unbreakable bond of marriage. The rings are blessed over the heads of the bride and groom three times and then are placed on the fourth finger of the right hand. The best man exchanges the rings three times, taking her ring and placing it on his finger, and vice-versa. The Betrothal ends with a prayer that God may strengthen the couple's union in faith, truth and love, and make them of one mind; and that He might grant them blessings.

The bride and groom are given lighted candles to hold, symbolizing that their lives should shine with virtue.

Three long prayers are read asking God to grant the bride and groom a long and peaceful mutual love and understanding, happiness and health, and the right hands of the couple are joined by the priest, who calls upon God "to join your servants, unite them in one mind and one flesh."

The most visible ceremony of the marriage service proper is the crowning of the bride and groom with two crowns or wreaths linked by a silken ribbon. The priest raises the crowns and makes the sign of the cross three times over the heads of the bride and groom, after which the best man places them on their heads, swapping them around three times. The crowning signifies that the newly married couple receive the grace of the Holy Spirit to be the founders of a new generation and are crowned with virtue and holiness to live their lives to the glory of God.

Above: The betrothal
Below: The best man repeatedly swaps the crowns during the prayers

The rite of crowning is followed by the reading of the Epistle and Gospel. The Gospel reading describes the marriage at Cana of Galilee which was attended and blessed by Christ, and His first miracle. After the Bible readings the bride and groom each drink wine three times from a single cup, whichsymbolizes their future common life together, and that the couple must share their joys and sorrows.

The custom has grown up in recent years among young women, that at the point when the words being chanted in the service say that "the woman shall fear the man," the bride stamps her foot on the bridegroom's toes to signify that she does not intend to take a subordinate position in the marriage.

While hymns are chanted, the priest takes the bride and groom by the hand and leads them around the small table three times, signifying the eternity of the bond between the couple, in what is popularly known as the "dance of Isaiah". The husband and wife are taking their first steps together as a married couple, and the

Above: The "Dance of Isaiah"
Below: Bride and groom at the table bearing the sweets which will be offered to the guests

Church, in the person of the priest, leads them in the way they should go. As they process around, those present throw rice over them as a symbol of fruitfulness. Finally, the priest blesses the couple and lifts the crowns from their heads.

The traditional Greek wedding reception is usually a huge party, which in past ages went on for several days and nights, and even today can last through the night.

Divorce and remarriage is allowed by the Orthodox Church, this being seen as a necessary concession to human frailty. A second, and even a third marriage is permitted; but under no circumstances, not even death, is a fourth ever countenanced.

Holy Orders

Members of the Church believe that the mission and authority of teaching (*magisterium*) and the power of conferring grace was committed by Christ to His apostles, who were to continue His work on earth as His earthly representatives. The apostles received this power from Christ, and they passed on this mission and power in its fullness to others in the Church, known as bishops, in unbroken succession. This, the bishops have passed on to others in unbroken succession from the time of the apostles by the sacrament of ordination. A limited portion of their mission and powers they also give to others: priests and deacons, although these are not allowed to pass on the gifts they have received to others. The Orthodox regard this hierarchical constitution of the Church, with its various degrees and orders, as an essential part of its structure.

Thus the Orthodox recognise the traditional threefold ministry of bishop, priest and deacon, conferred by ordination, which goes back to the earliest days of the Church. There are many other ranks in the clerical hierarchy: patriarchs, archbishops, archpriests, archimandrites, etc. These receive no special ordination, but merely possess some higher rank or greater dignity than others belonging to the same order. Only a bishop has the power to ordain, and the consecration of a new bishop must be performed by at least two bishops, never by one alone. The chief agents of the bishops are the priests, who have charge of most churches. They may be assisted by deacons. Below the diaconate are certain minor orders such as sub-deacons, doorkeepers and singers. A bishop administers all the sacraments; the priest all except Ordination; while the Deacon can only assist in the performance of the Liturgy and the Sacraments.

Ordination is said to be the consequence of a man receiving a call to become a clergyman and serve the spiritual needs of his fellow men and women. In order to be ordained a deacon, a man must be at least twenty-five years old. He must be thirty to be ordained a priest, and thirty-five to be consecrated a bishop.

In the Orthodox Church , a man with a vocation to the priesthood has the choice to be a married or a celibate clergyman. If married, he must get married before embarking upon the lowest level of ordination and cannot be remarried if he is subsequently widowed. If he marries, he cannot advance beyond the rank of priest. Second marriages are forbidden to clergy. After being widowed, however, when he is of mature age and his children have grown up, he may be tonsured as a monk, and in that way he may become a candidate for promotion to a bishopric. Bishops must be celibate, and their numbers are drawn from the unmarried priests attached to the monasteries. Thus an ambitious cleric will remain unmarried. (See below, Chapter 6)

The essential part of the sacrament of ordination is the physical laying on of hands upon the ordinands by the bishop, which takes place during the liturgy. The same form of words is used, with necessary adaptation, for deacons, priests and bishops. Thus for the ordination of a priest the formula is: "The grace of God, that always strengthens the weak and fills the empty, appoints the most religious deacon N. to be priest". Those being ordained receive ceremonially the vestments appropriate to their order from the ordaining bishop. The newly ordained priests and bishops then share in the celebration of the liturgy with the ordaining bishop(s).

Above: Bishops gathered with the archbishop of Athens for the consecration of a new bishop
Below: A new bishop receiving the greetings of his former parishioners and friends outside the cathedral of Athens

As the bishop vests the newly ordained or consecrated men, he holds up each of the vestments, saying in a loud voice, "*Axios!*" Then the choir sing, and the people shout, "*Axios!*" (He is worthy). This is a relic of a long-past democratic system whereby the people once elected their own bishops. Later it became the prerogative of prominent individuals who were patrons of their local church, who were granted virtually unconditional right to choose the bishop for that church. This did not accord with the desire of the emperors to control the leadership of the Church. The laws of Justinian of the mid-sixth century state that the right to choose a bishop did not belong to the people, but to the emperors and the clergy. In this way the people were gradually deprived of the rights of election. At the Second Ecumenical Council (381), it was decided that secular authorities had no right to elect the clergy: ". . . he who is raised to the episcopate must be chosen by bishops." Theoretically, however, the people can still cry *Anaxios*!" or "He is unworthy!"

The Roman Catholic Church recognizes the validity of Orthodox priestly orders, and a Catholic who is near death and unable to find a Catholic priest may make his confession to, and receive the sacraments from, an Orthodox priest.

The Anointing of the Sick

The anointing of the sick with oil is given to all who desire it, not just those in danger of death, as in the Roman Catholic Church. It can be repeated as often as circumstances dictate. The priest anoints the sick person on the forehead, nostrils, mouth, breast, and both sides of the hands. After this, holy communion is usually given.

Traditionally, the rite requires seven priests, seven readings from the epistles and gospels, seven prayers and seven anointings with oil specifically blessed for the service. Although it is not always possible to perform the sacrament in this way, the normal procedure is still to gather together as many priests as possible for this rite.

Funerals

The funeral service, although not considered as specifically sacramental, belongs among the special liturgical rites of the Church.

A special vigil to be said over the body of someone who has died takes the form of matins, and includes the *kontakion* of the dead, which is a meditation on the tragedy of death and the mercy of God, and a petition for eternal life for the person who is "fallen asleep."

"You only Creator Who with profound wisdom order all things mercifully, and give to all that which is useful, give rest, O Lord, to the soul of Your servant who has fallen asleep, for he has placed his trust in You, our Maker and Fashioner and our God.
With the saints give rest, O Christ, to the soul of Your servant where sickness and sorrow are no more, neither sighing, but life everlasting."

The hymn of Saint John of Damascus continues:

"What earthly sweetness remains unmixed with grief? What glory stands immutable on earth? All things are but feeble shadows, all things are most deluding dreams; yet one moment only, and death shall supplant them all. But in the light of Your countenance, O Christ, and in the sweetness of Your beauty, give rest to him whom You have chosen, forasmuch as You love mankind.
I weep and lament when I think upon death, and behold our beauty created in the likeness of God lying in the tomb disfigured, bereft of glory and form. O the marvel of it! What is this mystery concerning us? Why have we been delivered to corruption? Why have we been wedded to death?"

Parish churches are not normally surrounded by a graveyard. These ares usually situated on the edge of a town or village. The funeral service is held in a special mortuary chapel in the graveyard. It is sometimes the custom for the coffin to remain open until after the service, and the wreaths are carried to the grave from the chapel on long poles.

It is also a common practice to place a picture of the deceased on the grave, and great latitude is allowed in displaying mementoes of the dead.

Graves displaying mementos of the departed

Above: An ossuary in a public cemetery.
Above left: Most of the boxes are simply stored on shelves in a large ossuary.

Centuries of erosion have made deep earth in many parts of Greece a rarity, and burial space, particularly in the Greater Athens area, is at a premium. Unless a family owns a burial plot, the normal practice is to bury the dead in rented plots for a period of three years. After that time the body is exhumed. The relatives are expected to be present on this occasion, and if the body has decayed, the bones are stored in metal boxes and kept in ossuaries. Sometimes the corpse has not decayed, particularly if the deceased had received chemotherapy for cancer some time before death. In such cases the body has to be reburied for a further period of time.

Memorial service said at a graveside

Cremation is not allowed by the Greek Orthodox Church, on the grounds that the body is holy, and that human beings have no right to destroy what God has created and sanctified. At present a religious burial service conducted by a Greek Orthodox priest is the only legitimate way to dispose of the dead, since Greece does not yet possess a single state crematorium, and the Church is strongly against the establishment of one.

Short memorial services for the dead are performed by a priest at the graveside on the third, ninth and fortieth day of the anniversary of death. In addition, on four special "Soul Saturdays" during the course of each year, *kollyva,* made of boiled wheat and pomegranate seeds, is prepared and taken to church. Afterwards it is taken to the graveside, where some is sprinkled on the graves of the deceased, and some offered to passers-by.

5

The Annual Drama of Salvation

Half a century ago Peter Hammond wrote eloquently of the power of the Church calendar over the ordinary citizens of Greece:

"Nobody who has lived and worshipped amongst Greek Christians for any length of time but has sensed in some measure the extraordinary hold which the recurring cycle of the Church's liturgy has upon the piety of the common people. Nobody who has kept the great lent with the Greek Church, who has shared in the fast which lies heavy upon the whole nation for forty days; who had stood for long hours, one of an innumerable multitude who crowd the tiny Byzantine churches of Athens and over-flow into the streets, while the familiar pattern of God's saving economy towards man is re-presented in psalm and prophecy, in lections from the Gospel, and the matchless poetry of the canons; who has known the desolation of the holy and great Friday, when every bell in Greece tolls its lament and the body of the Saviour lies shrouded in flowers in all the village churches throughout the land; who has been present at the kindling of the new fire and tasted of the joy of a world released from the bondage of sin and death-none can have lived through all this and not have realised that for the Greek Christian the Gospel is inseparably linked with the liturgy that is unfolded week by week in his parish church. Not among the Greeks only but throughout Orthodox Christendom the liturgy has remained at the very heart of the Church's life."[1]

The years since those words were written have seen massive secularisation in Greece. Contact with foreigners through mass tourism, membership of the European Union, and the education of many middle-class Greeks abroad; the development of a materialistic consumer society, rising standards of living, and mass migration from the countryside into Athens, have all contributed to the breakdown of traditional patterns of behaviour. Well-to-do young people crowd into the fast-food outlets, and the wealthy into the expensive tavernas, in Lent no less than throughout the rest of the year. The rich move into their second homes, or holiday abroad over Easter. Yet Greeks have always displayed a unique ability to absorb the new and alien while losing little of their own distinctive traditions. And each year on Palm Sunday, the life of the nation is manifestly caught up once again in the events of the Passion and Resurrection of Christ, in a fashion that finds little parallel in Northern Europe, and none in North America. A few years ago this was symbolised for the author by the sight of the staff of the ubiquitous MacDonalds, and their Greek rivals next door, in the centre of the busy Athenian suburb of Nea Smyrni, lined up outside their empty premises, lighted candles in their hands, waiting for the passing of the bier of the dead Christ on the evening of Great Friday.

The Calendar

The Orthodox ecclesiastical year begins on September 1st. In addition to Easter, "the Feast of Feasts", there are twelve major feast days of the Church which are universally celebrated: the Nativity, *Theophania* (Epiphany), the Presentation in the Temple, the Transfiguration, the Entry into Jerusalem, and the Ascension of Christ; the feast of Pentecost (Whitsun Day); the Nativity, Annunciation, Presentation to the Temple and "Falling asleep" of Mary; and the Exaltation of the Cross.

As in the Western Churches, this calendar is made up of two series, one based upon the fixed dates of the calendar, and the other on the movable date of Easter. This is usually different from the date of the Western Easter. The same method of calculation is used in East and West: the first Sunday after the fourteenth day after the first new moon after March 6th. But the Orthodox Church uses the old Gregorian calendar in order to determine the date of March 6th, which is behind the Julian calendar, so that the Orthodox Easter usually falls later than the Western festival. The Sundays of the year are named after the subject of the Gospel passage read out on that day during the Liturgy, e.g. "the Sunday of the Prodigal Son," "the Sunday of the Myrrh-Bearers".

Although the Roman day began at midnight, the Jewish day begins at sunset, and for this reason, the vespers of the day before a feast takes on the character of that festival. Thus the services celebrating a particular feast begin on the preceding evening.

The Annunciation

The feast of the Annunciation of the Virgin Mary falls nine months before Christmas day, on the twenty-fifth of March. It is the celebration of the announcement of the conception of Christ to the Virgin Mary as recorded in the Gospel of Saint Luke. The services of the day stress again and again the joyous news of salvation:

> "Today is the beginning of our salvation, the revelation of the eternal mystery. The Son of God becomes the Son of the virgin, as Gabriel announces the coming of Grace. Together with him let us cry to the Mother of God: Rejoice, Full of Grace, the Lord is with you."

In Greece this March 25th is also the day on which the struggle for independence was launched. Consequently, it is now celebrated as the National Holiday with military parades. In this the close association between Church and state can be observed. It is a celebration both of the good news of the Conception of Christ and of the Nation. Religious, political and military authorities preside together over the occasion, when a solemn doxology or act of thanksgiving is made in the Athens Cathedral in the presence of the President and the members of the Government and armed forces.

The Mid-Winter Festivals

Three important festivals occur during mid-Winter: Christmas Day, Saint Basil's Day (New Year's Day), and Theophania (Epiphany).

Christmas Day does not have the pre-eminence among Christian holy days in Greece which it has in the West, and it takes a place much inferior to Easter. It was a late introduction into the East from the Western Church, and did not really catch the public imagination until recently. Saint Basil's Day, or New Year's Day, is still probably more important in the public mind as. It is on Saint Basil's Day that, traditionally, Greek children received presents.

Theophania, known in the West as Epiphany, was originally the day on which the birth of Christ, as well as his baptism in the Jordan, was commemorated. It remains even today the chief celebration of the Incarnation. The baptism by John in the Jordan is the central epiphany glorified in the main hymns of the feast:

> "When You, O Lord, were baptized in the Jordan the worship of the Trinity was made manifest! For the voice of the Father bare witness to You, calling You his Beloved Son. And the Spirit, in the form of a dove, confirmed the truthfulness of his Word. O Christ our God, who has revealed Yourself and hast enlightened the world, glory to You.
> Today You have appeared to the universe, and Your Light, O Lord, has shone on us, who with understanding praise You: You have come and revealed Yourself, O Light Unapproachable!"

On the day before this festival, priests take holy water round to all dwelling houses and apartments in their parishes to bless them. This is known as the "Little Blessing of the water". On the day of Theophania itself, at the end of the Liturgy there takes place the "Great Blessing of the waters".

The "Greater Blessing" follows the Divine Liturgy. It begins with the singing of special hymns and the censing of the water which has been placed in the centre of the church building. Surrounded by candles and flowers, this water stands for the world of God's creation. The celebrant immerses the Cross into the water three times and then sprinkles the water to the four points of the compass. He then blesses the people with the sanctified water. After holy water has been blessed in the churches, it is available to members of the congregation to take home. On the seacoast, or where there is a lake, river, reservoir, or even a swimming bath, the waters are blessed again in a striking public ceremony. The bishop, clergy and congregation move to the edge of the waters, and at its blessing, the bishop throws into it a wooden cross, and the young men dive in to retrieve it. It is considered a great honour to be the one who returns it to the bishop.

At this ceremony is sung the great poem of Patriarch Sophronius of Jerusalem. I shall quote from this at some length because it demonstrates many of the characteristics of the liturgical poetry of the Orthodox Church. With its reiterated "today" it demonstrates the sense of the Orthodox that the worship of the Church "makes present" the events of salvation, which have both historical and eternal aspects to them:

A vat ready for the blessing of the water on Theophania

> "Today the hour of our festival has come, and the choir of the saints assists with us, and angels celebrate together with men. Today the grace of the Holy Spirit, in the

form of a dove, has descended upon the waters. Today the sun, which knows no setting, has arisen, and the world is illuminated with the light of the Lord. Today the moon with shining rays shines forth upon the world. Today the glowing stars adorn the universe with the splendour of their lustre. Today the clouds refresh mankind by raining down righteousness from heaven."

As this hymn continues, it focuses upon the fundamental Christian belief that the at a particular time the eternal God became man, and does so by developing many of the fundamental paradoxes inherent in this idea:

Above: The archbishop blessing the water at on the seafront, at suburban Glyfada, outside Athens
Below: Young people race to recover the cross

"Today He Who is uncreated endures the laying on of hands from him whom He had formed. Today the prophet and forerunner approaches the Master, but is seized with fear, seeing the condescension of God for us. Today the streams of Jordan are changed into healing waters by the presence of the Lord. Today all creation is watered with mystic waves. Today the offences of men are washed away by the waters of Jordan.

Today Paradise is opened to men, and the Sun of Righteousness has illuminated us. Today the bitter water of the people of Moses becomes most sweet from the presence of the Lord. Today we are released from our ancient woe, and we find salvation as the new Israel. Today we are redeemed from darkness and illumined by the light of the knowledge of God. Today the gloom of the world is cleared away by the manifestation of our God. Today all creation is made bright from on high. Today error has been overcome and our way of salvation has been made smooth by the coming of the Master. Today the things above celebrate with those below, and the things below confer with those above. Today the holy assembly of the faithful sounds forth their joy. Today the Master pleads for Baptism, in order that He may lift mankind on high. Today He Who stoops not, stoops down to His own servant, that we may be freed from bondage. Today we have been purchased for the Kingdom of Heaven, for of the kingdom of the Lord there shall be no end. Today earth and sea share the joy of the world, and the world has been filled with gladness."

As always, Orthodox liturgical poetry demonstrates awareness of the divinity of Christ, hidden by his humanity:

"The waters saw You, O God, the waters saw You and were afraid. Jordan was driven back when it saw the fire of the Godhead descending in bodily form and resting upon it. Jordan was driven back when it beheld the Holy Spirit in the form of a dove descending, and hovering around You. Jordan was driven back when it saw the Unseen made visible, the Creator made incarnate, and the Master in the form of a servant. Jordan was driven back and the hills leaped when they looked down upon God in the flesh, and the clouds gave forth a voice marvelling at that which had come to pass: Light from Light, true God from true God."

Great Lent

The greatest festival of the year, Easter, is preceded both by a period of preparation for Lent and by the forty days of strict fasting in Lent itself, which begins on "Clean Monday", which corresponds to the Western "Ash Wednesday".

The Eastern Church is much more rigorous about the discipline of fasting than is the Western Church. In Greece, many people who are not otherwise very observant in their religious practices, nevertheless use Lent as a form of purging, in the belief that the fast is a traditional way of giving the body a change from its usual diet, and a time to allow the build-up of poisons which accumulate in the body to be cleared away. Although the full fast begins on Clean Monday, Greeks traditionally abstain from meat for one week before that. The full Lenten fast includes cheese, butter and eggs.

The Vesper service which begins the Lenten season is called the "Vespers of Forgiveness". It is customary at this service for the congregation to ask each other's forgiveness, and mutually to forgive each other.

The weekday services of Great Lent are characterized by special melodies of a penitential character. The central doorway leading to the sanctuary remains closed to signify man's separation through sin from God. The vestments worn are usually purple.

On the first Sunday in Lent the feast of Orthodoxy is celebrated. During the eighth and ninth centuries the Orthodox Church was rent by a bitter struggle between those who venerated images, and puritans who wished to abolish them altogether, known as the Iconoclastic Controversy. When, on February 19th, 843, the devotees of the icons triumphed, throughout that night of a thanksgiving was chanted by the people of Constantinople at the shrine of the Virgin at Blachernae, and then the people marched with lighted candles to complete their rejoicing in *Ayia Sophia*. On this day, at the conclusion of the morning service, all the portable icons are processed around the outside of the church in celebration of the triumph of the images.

On the evenings of the first five Fridays in Lent, a very popular and singularly beautiful service is held in most of the churches. In the space before the icon screen stands an icon of the Virgin Mary, beautifully decorated with flowers. The service is built around the veneration of this icon, and the singing of the *Akathistos Hymnos:* the hymn which must be sung standing. This hymn consists of twenty-four verses, one for each letter of the Greek alphabet. Each line begins with the salutation "Hail" (*Haire*) followed by a poetic title of the Virgin Mary. From this, the entire service is usually known as the *Haeritismoi*.

The *Haeritismoi* proper begin with the words: "A captain of the angels was sent from heaven to cry to the Virgin Mary "Hail!" And seeing you, Lord, become body, he stood marvelling, and with his bodiless voice cried out to her, saying…" There follow the series of salutations, each beginning "Hail!" each one of which is a commentary on the mystery of the Incarnation, as usual, bringing out the paradoxes which that doctrine entails:

"Hail, You through whom joy shall shine forth…
Hail, Height hard to climb for human minds.
Hail, Depth hardly visible to the eyes of the angels…
Hail, You Who are the throne of a king.
Hail, You Who sustained the Sustainer of all things.
Hail, Star that caused the Sun to appear.
Hail, Womb of the divine Incarnation.
Hail, unwedded Bride."

This long hymn is divided into four separate sections, one section is sung on each of the first four Fridays of Lent, and the entire hymn is sung on the fifth.

Immediately before and after the *Akathistos Hymnos,* is sung the beloved and melodious anthem "Invincible Commander". The citizens of Constantinople originally composed this to the Virgin Mary in a single night. In 626 AD the city was besieged by a large Persian force backed up by a fleet. When the Persian soldiers declared that they saw the figure of a woman clothed in garments of light walking on the walls surrounding the city, they turned and fled. At the same time, a sudden storm blew up, which wrecked their fleet. Led by the Patriarch Sergius, the people of the city crowded into one of the churches, and, it is said, spontaneously composed and sang this hymn: "Invincible Commander, Defender, to You do I, Your City, offer thank offerings for victory; for You, Mother of God, have delivered me from terror. And as you possess unconquerable power, free me from danger of every kind, that I may continue to cry to you: Hail, Unwedded Bride!" This anthem, which has become almost an anthem of the Greek Orthodox Church, is also sung on many other solemn occasions. After the singing of the *akathistos hymnos* the clergy and people queue up to venerate the icon of the Virgin.

On the eve of the celebration of the Resurrection of Lazarus, the forty days of Great Lent are brought to an end.

The service of Lazarus Saturday, commemorating Jesus' raising of Lazarus from the dead, is an anticipation of Easter.

"By raising Lazarus from the dead before Your Passion, You confirmed the universal resurrection, Christ our God! Like the children with the branches of victory, we cry out to You, O Vanquisher of Death: Hosanna in the highest! Blessed is he who comes in the name of the Lord!

Christ, the Joy, the Truth and the Light of all, the Life of the world and its Resurrection, has appeared in his goodness to those on earth. He has become the Image of our Resurrection, granting divine forgiveness to all."

Great Week

At the church service on the morning of Palm Sunday, the churches may be decorated with palms or other branches, and the members of the congregation are presented with sprigs of myrtle or bay; however, there is no solemn procession as there is in Roman Catholic countries. Nevertheless, the hymns for the day resound with echoes of Christ's triumphal entry into Jerusalem.

"Today the grace of the Holy Spirit has gathered us together. Let us all take up Your cross and say: Blessed is he who comes in the name of the Lord. Hosanna in the highest!

When we were buried with Thee in baptism, O Christ our God, we were made worthy of eternal life by Thy resurrection. Now we praise Thee and sing: Hosanna in the highest! Blessed is he who comes in the name of the Lord!

Sitting on Thy throne in heaven, and carried on a foal on earth, O Christ our God, accept the praise of angels and the songs of children who sing: Blessed is he who comes to recall Adam!"

The church service on the evening of Palm Sunday is the first of a series that continue throughout Great Week, the theme of which is the passion, or suffering, of Christ. Standing before the congregation in the space before the icon screen is displayed the icon of Christ crowned with thorns. From the anthem "Behold the bridegroom comes in the middle of the night" which is sung at these services, they are known as Bridegrooms (*Nymphyoi*):

"Behold the Bridegroom comes in the middle of the night, and blessed is the servant whom he shall find watching; and unworthy is he whom he shall find heedless. Beware, therefore, O my soul, lest you be borne down with sleep, lest you be given up to death, and lest you be shut out from the kingdom. Wherefore rouse yourself and cry: 'Holy, holy, holy are You, our God; through the protection of the heavenly hosts, save us.'" Later this theme is repeated: "I see your bridal chamber adorned, O my Saviour, but I have no wedding garment that I may enter. O Giver of Light, make radiant the vesture of my soul, and save me."

The service on Monday is based upon the parable of the wise virgins who, unlike their foolish sisters, were ready when the Lord came to them.

On Tuesday evening On Tuesday the focus is on Mary Magdalene, the fallen woman who repented, anointing of the feet of Christ. This sinful harlot who was saved is contrasted with Judas, the chosen apostle who was lost. During this service the famous Hymn of Kassiane is sung.

"Woe to me!" she said, "for my night is an ecstacy of excess, gloomy, moonless and full of sinful desire. Receive the springs of my tears, you who gather into clouds the waters of the sea. In your ineffable condescension, deign to bow Yourself down to me and to the lamentations of my heart. I will fervently embrace your sacred feet, and wipe them with the tresses of the hair of my head. Your feet, at whose sound Eve hid herself for fear when she heard you walking in Paradise in the cool of the day..."

The Kassiane who wrote this hymn was a candidate for the hand in marriage of the emperor Theophilos, but not being chosen, she became a nun. In 859, she wrote the hymn which subsequently made her famous.

There is no service on Wednesday evening. Instead, the Service of General Holy

Unction takes place, usually in the late afternoon. The priest makes the sign of the Cross with consecrated oil on the forehead of each member of the congregation, especially the sick and the very young. It is a preparation for those who are to receive Holy Communion on the next day or during the Easter period.

The services on the morning of Great Thursday commemorate the Last Supper and the betrayal of Christ.

"When Your glorious disciples were enlightened at the washing of their feet before the supper, then the impious Judas was darkened by the disease of avarice, and to the lawless judges he betrayed You, the Righteous Judge. Behold, O lover of money, this man because of avarice hanged himself. Flee from the insatiable desire which dared such things against the Master! O Lord who deals righteously with all, glory to You."

The following is sung at the Liturgy:

"Of Your mystical supper, O Son of God, accept me today a communicant, for I will not speak of Your mystery to Your enemies, neither like Judas will I give You a kiss, but like the thief will I confess You: Remember me, O Lord, in Your kingdom."

The services on the morning of Great Thursday commemorate the Last Supper and the betrayal of Christ. In just a few places, such as the island of Patmos, there is a special commemoration of Jesus' washing the feet of his disciples.

The long service in the evening of Thursday contains twelve gospel readings, which narrate Christ's crucifixion. Following the fifth reading (usually some time after 8:30 pm), a large cross bearing a two dimensional image of Christ and adorned with lighted candles is brought into the nave of the church in solemn procession, and then carried three times around the space in front of the entrance to the sanctuary, to the tolling of the church bells. At the same time the following verse is sung:

"Today is hung upon the tree He who suspended the land in the midst of the waters. A crown of thorns crowns Him Who is the King of the angels. He is wrapped about with the purple robe of mockery, Who wrapped the heavens with clouds..."

Since the service takes place at the same time everywhere in each town and city, at this time, as this point is reached in the service, church bells will begin to toll from every direction. The cross is then set up in the centre of the *solea*, and venerated by the congregation. In some places, a vigil is kept in the church throughout the night.

During the morning service, the wooden pegs representing nails holding the figure of Christ on the cross are knocked out. The figure of Christ is then taken down from the cross and wrapped in a white cloth. This usually takes place at about 10.30 am. Outside the church, the women have decorated with flowers a bier upon which a representation of the dead Christ will be carried. This decorated bier is brought into the church. Finally, a large piece of cloth, embroidered with the image of the dead Christ and known as the *epitaphio*, is brought out into the nave of the church carried by all the priests, usually held over their heads. As it is processed around the nave, the congregation throw flower petals scented water over it. At the same time the bells begin to toll, and the national flags on all public buildings throughout the country are taken down to half-mast.

Meanwhile, outside the church, the women have decorated with flowers a bier, which is carried into the church. Finally, a large piece of cloth, embroidered with the image of the dead Christ and known as the *epitaphio*, is brought out from the sanctuary into the nave of

Left: Taking Christ dowwn from the cross, on the morning of Great Friday
Right: Priest bringing the epitafio, which represents the dead Christ,
into the body of the church, on the morning of Great (Good) Friday

the church carried by all the priests, usually held over their heads. As it is processed around the nave, the members of the congregation throw flower petals and scatter scented water over it. At the same time the bells in all the churches begin to toll, and the national flags on all public buildings throughout the country are lowered to half-mast.

The evening service of Great Friday takes the form of a burial service. At this time the large cross standing in the space before the icon screen bears only the crown of thorns. In front of it, the *epitaphio,* representing the dead Christ lies on its flower-decorated bier, where it has been visited by worshippers throughout the day. The focus of the service is this representation of the dead Christ. It typically focuses upon the paradox of the death of One who was both God and man: "Be amazed O heaven, and let the foundations of the earth quake; for He who dwells in the highest has been accounted among the dead, and has been a guest in a humble tomb."

The poetry of the Lamentations which are sung alternates between tender compassion and wonder at the mystery of Redemption. Again the many paradoxes inherent

The epitafio on its flower-bedecked bier, Great Friday

in the idea of the Incarnation are drawn out in detail:

"O Christ, the Life, you were laid in the tomb, and armies of angels were amazed, and they glorified your condescension.

O Life, how can You die? How can You dwell in the tomb? You break down the kingdom of Death, and raise up those who were dead in Hades.

You, Jesus, King of all, set the measurements of the earth, yet today You dwell in a narrow grave...

You, O Christ the Life, were laid in the tomb, and by Your death You destroyed Death and shed life upon the world...

Both the Mind of Nature and the angelic hosts are at a loss to understand the mystery, O Christ, of Your ineffable and inexplicable burial.

O strangest of miracles! O latest of happenings! He Who gave me breath, is carried away bereft of breath, and is buried by the hands of Joseph. When You, O Christ the Fashioner, were laid in the tomb, the foundations of Hades were shaken and the graves of mortals were opened.

The earth shuddered and the sun hid itself, when You, O Christ the Saviour, the unwaning Light, did in the flesh sink down into the grave.

You had neither form nor comeliness, O Word ... in Your sufferings, but rising up You have illuminated and beautified mortals with Divine radiance...

The procession of the epitafio, on the evening of Great Friday

The sun darkened his light and shuddered when he saw You, O Christ, the unseen Light, bereft of breath, and hidden in the grave...

The women came with myrrh, to anoint Christ the Anointed.

The deceiver has been deceived, and he who is deceived is redeemed by Your Wisdom, O my God.

O Son of God, the King of all, my God and Fashioner, how have you endured suffering?"

The lamentations also dwell upon the suffering of Jesus' Mother, at the foot of the Cross:

"Your pure mother wept bitter tears over You, O Jesus, and she cried: 'How can I lay You, my Son, in the grave?

Who will give me water and a fountain of tears,' exclaimed the divinely-wed Virgin, 'that I may weep for my beloved Jesus?'...

O God, the eternal Word, beyond description, Your pure Mother, beholding You in a Tomb, wept bitterly.

When Your all-pure Mother beheld Your death, O Christ, she cried out with bitterness: 'Tarry not, O Life, among the dead.'...

'O my sweet spring-time, my most beloved Child, whither has Your beauty sunk down?' Your all-holy Mother was moved to tears, when You die, O Word.

The fearful Hades trembled when it saw You, O Immortal Sun of Glory, and in haste gave up its captives.

Now all the faithful, who were redeemed from death by the Tomb, extol with hymns Your Crucifixion and Your Tomb, O Christ...

The Mother cried aloud when she saw her Son hanging on the Tree.

The Maiden pierced to the heart, cried out in her fervent weeping.

'O Light of my eyes, my beloved Boy, how are You now hidden in the grave?'

I glorify, O my Son, Your deep compassion, on account of which You suffer these things.

Arise, O Merciful Master, and raise us up from the chasm of Hades.

Your Mother, who bore You, cried out weeping: 'Arise, O giver of Life.'"

Usually at about 9.00 pm, although there are great local variations, the flower decorated bier, with the *epitaphio* on it, is taken out of the church in solemn procession. The people inside and outside the church follow behind this funeral procession carrying candles of unbleached brown wax. At the cathedral in Athens and at other cathedrals, the procession takes the form of a full state funeral, accompanied by soldiers or sailors bearing reversed arms, and followed by high officers of state and the armed forces. The evening service takes the form of a funeral service. At this time the large cross standing in the space before the icon screen carries only the crown of thorns. In front of it, the *epitaphio,* or embroidered cloth representing the dead Christ, lies on its flower-decorated bier.

On the morning of Great Saturday, at the service of the "First Resurrection", the priest emerges from the icon screen with a basket of bay leaves. He scatters them over the congregation, chanting "Arise, O God, to judge the world." At this point great noise is sometimes made in the church to represent the shaking of Hades at Christ's resurrection.

During the early evening of this day, the Holy Fire from the Resurrection service at the Church of the Holy Sepulchre in Jerusalem arrives at Athens airport on an Olympic Airways jet accompanied by a government minister. The sacred flame is conveyed to the church and residence of the representative of the Patriarch of Jerusalem in the Plaka, and from there the fire is taken to the various cities and towns of Greece for use in the midnight Resurrection service.

Virtually the entire country is present at a church for the announcing of the Resurrection of Christ at midnight on Easter Day – the climactic moment of the festive year.

The service begins at 11.00. At a certain point in the proceedings, all lights in the church are extinguished. Then the priest appears at the royal doors in the icon screen with a candle lit from the holy fire, and sings: "Come and take light from the Undying Light, and glorify Christ, who has risen from the dead." The congregation crowd forward to light their own white candles from his taper. Then all go outside the church, where everyone else is assembled, when the flame is passed on to them.

On top of the church steps outside the doors, or on a specially erected platform in front of the church, the gospel account of the discovery of the empty tomb is read out, ending just prior to midnight. At the stroke of midnight exactly, the priest begins to intone the Paschal anthem: "Christ is risen from the dead, by his death trampling on death; and to those in the tombs he has given life." The bells ring out and firecrackers are let off. In harbours, the ships sound their sirens. Families, friends and acquaintances wish each other a happy Easter, usually using the traditional greeting *Christos anesti* ("Christ is risen,") with the reply *Alithos*

The commemoration of the Resurrection

anesti ("He is truly risen)." As the crowds depart, the devout go back into the church for the rest of the Easter liturgy.

The services of Great Thursday, Friday and Saturday are a dramatic ritual re-enactment of the death, burial and resurrection of Christ. But they are intended to be much more than that. They are a setting out of the inner spiritual and eternal meaning of the saving events of Christ, as understood by the Church which possesses the full knowledge of their significance and power. For that reason, there is no dramatic pretence that the outcome of these events is unknown. The Church does not sorrow and mourn over Jesus without the awareness of the significance of his suffering. Throughout the services the victory of Christ is contemplated and the resurrection is proclaimed, since it is held that it is only in the light of the Resurrection that the eternal meaning of the events of Christ's passion and death can be properly appreciated and understood.

The Feasts of the Virgin

The main theme of the feast of Mary's entrance to the Temple, repeated many times in the services, is the fact that she enters the Temple to become herself the living temple of God, thus inaugurating the New Testament in which are fulfilled the prophecies of old that "the dwelling of God is with man" and that the human person is the sole proper dwelling place of the Divine Presence.

"Today is the preview of the good will of God, of the preaching of the salvation of mankind. The Virgin appears in the temple of God, in anticipation proclaiming Christ to all. Let us rejoice and sing to her: Rejoice, O Divine Fulfilment of the Creator's dispensation.

The most pure Temple of the Saviour, the precious Chamber and Virgin, the Sacred Treasure of the Glory of God, is presented today to the house of the Lord. She brings with her the grace of the Spirit, which the angels of God do praise. Truly this woman is the Abode of Heaven!"

The feast of the "Dormition" or Falling-asleep of the Mother of God is celebrated on the fifteenth of August, preceded by a two-week fast. This feast, which corresponds to the Catholic feast of the Assumption, commemorates the death, resurrection and glorification of Christ's mother. It proclaims that Mary has been "assumed" by God into the heavenly kingdom of Christ in the fullness of her spiritual and bodily existence.

As with the nativity of the Virgin and the feast of her entrance to the temple, there are no biblical or historical sources

The procession of the icon of the Panayia of Tinos on August 15th

for this feast. The Tradition of the Church is that Mary died as all people die, not "voluntarily" as her Son, but by the necessity of her mortal human nature which is indivisibly bound up with the corruption of this world.

The Orthodox Church teaches that Mary is without personal sins. In the Gospel of the feast, however, in the liturgical services and in the icon of the Falling Asleep, the Church proclaims as well that Mary truly needed to be saved by Christ as all human persons are saved from the trials, sufferings and death of this world; and that having truly died, she was raised up by her Son as the Mother of Life and participates already in the eternal life of paradise.

"In giving birth, you preserved your virginity. In falling asleep you did not forsake the world, O Theotokos. You were translated to life, O Mother of Life, and by your prayers, you deliver our souls from death.

Neither the tomb, nor death, could hold the Theotokos, who is constant in prayer and our firm hope in her intercessions. For being the Mother of Life, she was translated to life, by the One who dwelt in her virginal womb."

Holy Cross Day

The Elevation of the Cross, celebrated on the fourteenth of September, commemorates the finding of Christ's Cross by Saint Helen, the mother of the Emperor Constantine in the fourth century; and, after it was taken by the Persians, of its recovery by the Emperor Heraclius in the seventh century at which time it was "elevated" in the Church of the Resurrection in Jerusalem. From this latter event the "universal elevation" of the Cross was celebrated annually in all of the churches of the Christian Empire.

The day of the Elevation of the Cross became the national holiday of the Byzantine Empire. The Cross, the official emblem of the Empire which was placed on all public buildings and uniforms, was officially elevated on this day by the bishops and priests. They blessed the four directions of the universe with the Cross, while the faithful repeated the chant *Kyrie eleison*, ("Lord have mercy.") This ritual is still performed in the churches today after the solemn presentation and elevation of the Cross at the end of the vigil service of the holy day. The priest takes a cross, set up on a platter with sprays of basil, and holding it above his head he brings it into the body of the church, places it upon a table in the *solea,* and incenses it. Then he holds up the platter with the cross and having blessed the people with it, prostrates himself before it facing north, while *Kyrie eleison* ("Lord have mercy") is sung onehundred times. In turn, he faces east, north, west, south and east again, and while a hundred more *Kyrie eleisons* are sung each time.

The hymn of the feast which was sung on all public occasions in the Christian Empire of Byzantium, originally petitioned God to save the people, to grant victory in war and to preserve the empire "by the virtue of the Cross." Today the hymns of the day, are "spiritualised" as the "adversaries" have become the spiritually wicked and sinful including the devil and his armies, and "Orthodox Christians" replace the names of ruling officials of the Empire.

> "O Lord, save Your people and bless Your inheritance. Grant victories to the Orthodox Christians over their adversaries; and by the virtue of Your Cross, preserve Your habitation.
> As You were mercifully crucified for our sake, grant mercy to those who are called by Your name; make all Orthodox Christians glad by Your power, granting them victories over their adversaries, by bestowing on them the invincible trophy, Your weapon of peace."

Paneyiria

On each day of the year the Orthodox Church commemorates certain saints or sacred events in its history. In addition to the major feast days mentioned above, the entire Orthodox Church celebrates a number of other days with special liturgical and spiritual solemnity. In addition to the well-known saints, thus there exist others which are celebrated with great solemnity in just a very few places, perhaps even in just one particular place where they may have a special importance for the faithful.

Every Greek church is dedicated to a mystery of the Christian religion or to a saint, and celebrates with special observances on the day before and the day marked in the church calendar for that mystery or saint. Some small churches are only used on that one day in the year. These festivals are called *paneyiria.* The form of celebration varies. Typically, although not invariably, on the day before there will be vespers in the church probably followed by a procession bearing the icon of the patronal saint or mystery. On the morning of the day proper there will be a liturgy in the church, followed in the evening by a communal feast with music and dancing. A small *paneyri* may have no procession or feast. A large one will last for three days, and people will flock from distant villages to join in the merry-making.

The many important saints days are not, in Greece, unnoticed by the general population. Because Greeks observe their name days rather than their birthdays, everyone knows when it is Saint Nicholas' Day, or Saint Spyridon, or a host of other saints' days, in a way that would be unthinkable elsewhere.

In addition to these special observances, each day of the week also has its special character. Sunday is always a commemoration of the Resurrection of Christ. On Wednesdays and Fridays Christ's suffering and crucifixion are recalled. Monday is dedicated to the angels, Tuesday to John the Baptist, Thursday to the apostles and St. Nicholas, and Saturday to the Mother of God and the departed.

The Service Books

Numerous different books are necessary to perform the services on the different holy days. There are eleven chief books. The *Typikon* is a perpetual calendar containing lists of the all the feasts, together with special arrangements for every possible coincidence. Each special office is listed, and the first words of all the lessons and hymns are given. The *Triodion* contains the Divine Office for the movable days from the tenth Sunday before Easter until Great Saturday; the *Pentekostarion* continues from Easter Day until All Saints' Sunday (the first after Pentecost); the *Oktoechos* has the offices for the Sundays during the rest of the year; the *Parakletike* has the week-day offices. The twelve *Menaias*, one for each month, give the lives of the Saints of the day, with their special hymns and prayers. The *Menologion* is an abbreviated summary of these. The *Horologion* contains the day-hours and the chief feasts from the *Menologion*. The *Psalter, Gospel* and *Apostle* contain the parts of the Bible read during the services.

6

Spiritual Shepherds

The clergy of the Orthodox Church, as those in the Roman Catholic Church, are recognised as an elite, and treated as such. Priests are addressed as "Father," and bishops as "Master" (*despode*).

Chief among the bishops are the patriarchs, and the most prominent of these is the ecumenical patriarch of Constantinople. The ecumenical patriarchs have never claimed to be leaders of the whole Church. The bishop of Rome has been accorded by them a primacy of honour as *primus inter pares*, or first among equals, and would now be accepted as such, were he not in schism. But because he is, the ecumenical patriarch of Constantinople now acts as *primus inter pares* provisionally in his place.

The Orthodox bishop is the undisputed head of his diocese. His authority has never been eroded by interference from the popes and their bureaucracy as was that of bishops in the West. The Greek bishops has a smaller diocese to look after than his Western counterparts. They are chosen from among the ranks of the unmarried hieromonks, or priest monks.

There are two types of priest in the Orthodox Church, married and unmarried. Married priests were already married before they became priests, and are allowed to retain their wives after their ordination; for priests cannot marry *as* priests. The married priests have usually been poorly educated, and many have received no academic theological training at all. On the other hand, they are usually native to the places they serve; they frequently pursue a trade; and they are closely integrated into the community. Thus the married priests form a valuable bridge between the unmarried clergy and the laity, closing a gap, which bedevils the Roman Catholic Church.

In the Orthodox Church, the deacon is a familiar and important figure, but as in the Western Church, the diaconate is in practice usually considered only as a temporary stepping-stone to the priesthood, for few deacons remain at this level by choice for life.

It is often claimed that in the Orthodox Church, emphasis is laid upon the importance of the laity, who are no less necessary to the existence of the Church than the clergy. In reality, the laity participate very little in the administration of the Church. Each parish has its church council, presided over by the parish priest, but its members are chosen by the bishop, with or without consultation with the priest, and they have limited powers.

However, the laity in Greece do sometimes interest themselves in theology, which is not seen as an exclusive domain of the clergy. The majority of teachers of theology in the universities are laymen, and most of their students are not ordinands. Many go on to teach religion in the schools, and some become official lay preachers.

Organisation

The Church of Greece proper has jurisdiction over all the modern Greek state except Crete, the islands of the Eastern Aegean and Mount Athos. These remain under the direct administration of the Patriarchate of Constantinople. The parts of northern Greece which were incorporated into the Greek state in 1913 send representatives to the Synod in Athens, although they are nominally under the jurisdiction of the Patriarchate. The Ecumenical Patriarch now exercises jurisdiction only over those places, and over the Orthodox of Turkey and Finland, and various emigrant churches.

The Church of Greece is governed by its holy synod, presided over by the archbishop of Athens, which has its headquarters in the Petraki Monastery, in Kolonaki, Athens.

The Holy Synod, the governing body of the Greek Church

The Dress of the Clergy

The Greek clergy, wearing their distinctive clothes, or vestments, are frequently observed figures in the streets, on public transport, and in the *kafenions* across the country.

The basic dress of all clergy is identical. This consists of a long, narrow-sleeved inner garment called a *rason,* or cassock, often belted at the waist. This is essentially an under-garment. Over it is worn the outer *rason:* a fuller gown with wide sleeves. This is always made of black stuff, but the inner *rason* may be of various colours. The higher clergy tend to use purple or dark blue, while in the monasteries grey is frequently adopted.

Their chief headgear is a cylinder of stiffened cloth known as the *kalymmafkion.* That worn by the married clergy is surmounted by a narrow brim, while the monastic form

Above: priests
Below: a bishop
in outdoor dress

is brimless. In Greece all the bishops as well as monastic clergy not actually residing in a community, wear the former type of *kalymmafkion.* On formal occasions, a bishop or an archimandrite will wear a long black veil known as *the epanokalymmafkion* draped over the *kalymmafkion,*

Visitors to Greece will not fail to notice the ubiquitous beard which every Greek cleric possesses. Peter Hammond observes wryly: "the notion lingers on that in the divine economy there is some mysterious connection between the orthodoxy of an ecclesiastical personage and the length of his beard; a beardless bishop would be unthinkable."[1]

The sacerdotal vestments used at the liturgy and in processions are complex and magnificent. Despite their exotic appearance, Roman Catholics will find that they generally consist of the same items as those worn in the Roman Catholic Church until the Second Vatican Council. The vestments of the ministers of both churches are descended from the ordinary dress of a Roman magistrate, it is just that their shape and style has evolved differently in the different churches. Curiously, under the Byzantine emperors, the dress of the Eastern clergy at the liturgy was very restrained. Only after the fall of the City and the imposition of Turkish rule did sartorial magnificence become the norm. This is because the Church at that time inherited, or adopted, the grand style previously peculiar to Byzantine secular officials.

During services, clerics in minor orders wear the *sticharion,* a long shirt with sleeves, reaching to the feet and wrists, generally made of silk and embroidered at the bottom. This corresponds to the catholic alb. Over this they may have an orarion, or long strip of embroidered material, wound around them."

Acolytes

Left: The vestments of a priest, showing the sticharion, epitrachelion, epigonation and phainolion.

Right: The vestments of a bishop, showing the sticharion, epigonation, phainolion and omophorion.

A deacon's *sticharion* has short sleeves. As it is always visible, it is generally more richly ornamented than those of the bishop and priest. It looks very like the Western dalmatic. The chief sign of the deacon's office is his *oration*, or stole, which hangs from the left shoulder straight to the ground before and behind. It usually has the words "Holy, holy, holy" embroidered on it. Whenever the deacon has to give a sign during the liturgy he takes the end of his *orarion* in the right hand and motions with it. When he goes to receive Holy Communion he winds it around his body.

Over his sticharion, the Priest wears a stole, called, in his case, an *epitrachelion*. It is worn round the neck and hangs down in front nearly to the feet. The two bands are generally hooked together or even permanently sewn up, leaving a loop through which he puts his head. It is ornamented with crosses or figures of saints and ends in fringes. The zone, or girdle, comes next. This is not a cord, as in the West, but a narrow belt joined by a clasp, and ornamented with crosses. It holds together the *epitrachelion* and *sticharion*. If a priest has been awarded any special honour, he also wears the *epigonation,* a strange lozenge-shaped object of stiff stuff, with a cross or image embroidered on it, which hangs at his right side from the girdle and reaches to the knee. It was originally a handkerchief, and corresponds to the Western maniple.

Over everything, the priest wears the *phainolion*. This outer garment is what in the West would be called a chasuble. It is was originally a great bell-shaped vestment with a hole cut in the centre, through which the head was put, reaching to the feet behind and at the sides, and lifted up in front by the arms. Since this could be inconvenient at the altar, in the Catholic Church the vestment came to be cut away at the sides to free the arms, although the fashion in recent years has been to return to the earlier form, using light material to facilitate more easy management. In the Orthodox Church the vestment has been cut away in front up to the waist for the same reason. The *phainolion* is also worn in processions, and so used as both a Western chasuble and as a cope.

A bishop wears his *sticharion*, which has red and white bands running from the shoulders to the feet. Over the wrists he then puts the *epimanikia*, a pair of cuffs, or long

*The priest's phainolion may be elaborate (left) for use at the liturgy
and in processions, or plain and simple for use in rituals (right)*

gloves with the part for the hand cut off, embroidered with crosses or holy images, corresponding to the Catholic bishop's gloves. The clumsiness of gloves has caused all of the cloth to be cut away in the Orthodox Church, except the wrist covering. Hanging from his *zone,* or belt, the bishop wears the *epigonation.*

As an outer garment, the bishop puts on the *sakkos,* a tunic reaching to below the knees, with short sleeves and divided up the sides, which are joined by bows of riband or clasps, and very richly embroidered. Originally only patriarchs wore the *sakkos,* while other bishops used the same phainolion (or chasuble) as priests. The *sakkos* was adopted at about the time of the fall of Constantinople. Over the *sakkos* comes the *omophorion* or pallium. The great *omophorion* is a wide band of silk or velvet embroidered with crosses and a lamb. The bishop passes it loosely round his neck, and one end hangs down in front (from the left side), the other behind. It is then kept in its place with ornamented pins. A smaller *omophorion* is worn during part of the liturgy, and for ordinations and other functions.

The Byzantine mitre is a gilt crown, ornamented with jewels and lined with red velvet. A bishop also wears a pectoral cross and a small medallion containing a relic. He carries a crozier which is shorter than that fashionable among Catholic bishops, and which ends in two branches curved round and ornamented with serpents' heads. Between them is a cross.

Above left: Bishop in full vestments
Right: Exarch of Cyprus wearing epanokalymmafkion
Below: episcopal crowns

When he gives his blessing at the end of the liturgy, a bishop holds in his right hand a triple candlestick with lighted candles, and a double one in his left. These candelabra stand for the two fundamental mysteries of the Orthodox faith: that the Godhead is three Divine Persons; and that Jesus Christ, the Saviour, has two natures, being both God and man.

These are the vestments used for the Liturgy and certain other great occasions. On less solemn occasions, such as the Divine Office, the bishop wears only the *mandyas*, or monastic cloak, *kalymmafkion, epanokalymmafkion,* and a smaller staff of wood with an ivory cross piece, like the letter "T".

7

Black Angels

The Origins of Monasticism

Monasticism originated in the desert of Egypt. There men fled the world to serve God in solitude, especially during times of persecution. The fame of St. Anthony (270-356) attracted many others, so that there were soon large colonies of monks, known as *laurai*. Each monk lived in his own hut, supporting himself under the direction of an older hermit, and meeting with the others on Saturdays and Sundays for public worship.

The monk was usually a layman; for while the clergy remained in the world and ministered to the people, the monk had renounced all intercourse with others. Later some monks were ordained in order to administer sacraments to their brethren, but even today the priest-monk (*ieromonachos*) is distinct from the normal monk, who is usually a layman.

Some rules of life for monks are attributed to Saint Pachomius, while others were developed by Saint Basil (330-379). Gradually nearly all the monasteries in the Byzantine Empire accepted the Rules of St. Basil. This laid down details of the various officials who would administer the monastery, the sequence of prayers, the frequency and nature of the meals, the types of work allowed, and punishments accorded to recalcritant individuals.

Since those early beginnings, monasticism has been very important feature of Orthodoxy throughout its history. But it has not branched into the various forms and varieties that make up the Roman Catholic religious life: with its mendicant friars, its teaching brothers, nursing sisters, etc. It still represents the system, or rather, that lack of system, that Saint Benedict found before he drew up his *Rule*. It has been said that an Orthodox monastery is the most perfect relic of the fourth century left in the world.

The Road to Heaven

Theoretically, at least, the purposes of entering a monastery are to repent of one's sins, to serve God according to the ideals of monastic asceticism, and to save one's soul.

There are four stages or ranks which Orthodox monks or nuns may pass through. The first step is that of novice, the rank of obedience. At this stage the candidate for monastic profession simply lives in the monastery under the direction of a spiritual father in obedience to the rule . He wears lay dress during this time. Three years is normally spent at this stage, although the period may be shortened for older people.

After the period of probation the monk receives a tonsure, a cassock, a leather belt, and a *kalymmafkion*. He is then accounted a *beginner*, and must grow a beard.

At the third level, after about two more years he makes solemn vows of poverty, chastity, and obedience, and receives a short cloak, the *mandyas*. The mandyas is the "angelic habit" that marks him out as a true monk. He also receives a new name. At this stage the new monk pledges to remain in the monastic community in perpetual obedience to the spiritual leader and to the head of the monastery, the abbot or abbess (*igoumenos* or *igoumenia*).

After some years more, some monks take a final step. This last stage is reserved for very few, since it is the entrance to the most strict observance of the monastic ideals, demanding normally a state of life in total seclusion in perpetual prayer and contemplation. With this final profession a new name is again received, and new monastic insignia, a great cloak marked with five crosses. This is a larger and more dignified cloak, distinguishing the elders of the monastery. Over time, the wearers of the great habit have come to form a superior class in the *lavra*.

There is no formally prescribed length of time that a person must remain in one or another of the monastic ranks. This is because of the personal, or individual nature of the monastic vocation. Some may progress rapidly, while others may take years, and still others may never be formally professed while still remaining within a monastic community. The decision is made on an individual basis by the abbot and the monk's spiritual director.

The Angelic Life

The basic idea of the Orthodox religious life is withdrawal from the world. As has been noted above. Most Orthodox monks are not usually priests, each monastery having only enough clergy to care for its own liturgical and sacramental requirements. That is the business of the bishops and secular clergy. Not are there any equivalent of the active orders in the Roman Catholic Church. Since monks "flee the world" they do not labour in it, even on works of charity. The main function of a monk is the worship of God. For this reason they are said to participate in the characteristic work of the angels. All monks sing the whole of their office every day in choir, and this takes up a great part of the day. On the eve of great feasts they may spend the whole night in the church keeping the vigil singing the office of the night-watch. The rest of the time they work for the monastery, as duties are apportioned to each by the abbot, the profits from which belong to the monastery. Men who already exercised a craft before entering the monastery may continue to exercise it as monks. Some practise medicine, study theology, calligraphy and painting. Many work the land in various ways.

There are some qualifications to this picture. Although the Orthodox Church does not have religious orders, different styles of monastic life have been developed in different monasteries. Some focus more upon the liturgy, others may be more ascetic; some have developed a mystical tradition, while others are inclined to spiritual guidance and openness to the world for the purpose of counselling or exorcism. But these various styles of vocation are not formalised.

Secondly, "technically" the bishops are chosen from among the ranks of the monks (but see below). In addition, historically, many missionaries and evangelists have been men with monastic vocations.

The monk has to abstain totally from meat at all times; his food being confined to fruit and vegetables and on feast-days fish, eggs, milk, and cheese. Wine is allowed. The chief meal, the only full meal in the day, is served at midday. On the frequent fast-days, including every Wednesday and Friday and the four periods of Lent, it is postponed until the ninth hour. (3 pm) Later in the evening, after compline, the remains of the meal are again spread in the refectory and any who wish, chiefly the younger members, might have a light supper.

Monastic Organisation

There have been three ways in which the monastic life has been organised among the Orthodox. The first is the eremitic life, where the individual monks or nuns live as hermits, anchorites or recluses, in total seclusion, never joining in the liturgical prayer of a community, except perhaps on the most solemn occasions.

In coenobitic monasteries, all members of the community live in common. In these, the monks possess nothing at all; live and eat together, and have definite tasks appointed to them by their superiors.

The third form was called idiorhythmic, in which the monks or nuns prayed together liturgically, but worked and ate individually or in small groups. In the *idiorythmic* monasteries the monks lived a more relaxed form of life. They dwelt entirely apart from one another and could own property. Each received from the monastery fuel, food and a very basic income, and the rest he had to earn for himself. These monks only met for the Divine Office and on great feasts for dinner. Otherwise, they lived independently.

This led to many abuses, some wealthy monks effectively functioning as businessmen. This form of monastic organisation has recently been abolished, the idiorythmic monasteries being converted to the coenobitic type.

Each monastery is independent, although most are under the jurisdiction of the metropolitan; and a few of the greatest are immediately subject to the patriarch, and for that reason are called *Stauropegia.* Many *lavras* have daughter-houses subject to their abbot. Such a dependent house is called a cell, or *kellion,* and these are sometimes grouped in a village called a *sketa.*

The head of a *lavra* is the *igoumenos* or "abbot". He is appointed by the metropolitan (or Patriarch); after having been elected by the monks, and is blessed and enthroned by him. He then rules for life, unless deposed for very scandalous conduct. The *igoumenos* has absolute authority over all his monks, but he is bound always by the rule of St. Basil, and he has to consult a committee of the more senior monks about all problems. This committee, the *synaxis,* limits the power of the superior.

The title "archimandrite" is given to abbots of the more important monasteries and also sometimes as a personal title of distinction.

A monk can receive permission from his abbot to take up the severer life of a hermit. He then goes to occupy a solitary cell near the *lavra.* He is still counted a member of the monastery and can return to it if he finds the solitary life unbearable. In the past, the drive of hermits to asceticism produced some exotic ways of life. Some hermits bound tight ropes around their bodies, or lived on the top of columns, such as Saint Simeon Stylites. There are still some genuine hermits in the Greek Church today, mostly living on Mount Athos.

Houses of Angels

The familiar tradition of monumental architecture characteristic of some Western religious orders, the Benedictines, Clunaics and Cistercians in particular, leads the visitor to expect the buildings of a Greek monastery to be magnificent edifices, and usually they are not. Some are old, and of historical importance, while others have fine paintings in their churches; but most are small and undistinguished. Until recent years, even great monasteries often had a curiously ramshackle aspect, and some still do.

The picturesque quality of many Greek monasteries usually lies not in the monumental character of the buildings, but in their being sited in inaccessible places.

> "Some of the most beautiful spots in Greece have been chosen for the situation of convents. In deep and secluded glens on the mountain's side, among trees of luxuriant foliage nourished by perennial waters, removed by the same elevation above the noisy disputes of the villagers and the noxious exhalations of the plains, the *caloyer* has little of earthly care or apprehension to direct his thoughts from the object they profess to prosecute..." (Waddington)

Typically, a monastery complex is built around an enclosed space. In the middle of this is a fountain and the main church, called the *katholicon*. On the ground floor of the enclosing building will be storerooms and offices, together with the refectory. On the floors above are the living quarters of the monks. In one corner of older monastic buildings there may be a keep, a defensible place of refuge in danger, containing the library. The older monasteries are frequently fortified, due mainly to the pirate raids which plagued the islands and shores of the Aegean until the nineteenth century.

Among the most spectacularly situated are the monastery of Saint Catherine, on the slopes of Mount Sinai, in Egypt, Megaspilion, in the northern Peloponnese, and Meteora, in Thessaly.

Above: Ayios
Mount Pendeli, Attica

Below: Monastery of Saint John the Forerunner, Makrinou, Megara

Bottom: Nea Moni, Chios

Above: Fortress monastery of the Apocalypse, Patmos

Below: Monastery of Saint George, Ilion, Euboeia

Bottom: Monastery of Vlacherna, Kanoni,, Corfu

Greek monks are to be found on the slopes of Mount Sinai in Egypt, where the Bible has it that Moses met God in the burning bush and where he received the ten commandments. To this place, it was said that angels carried the body of Saint Catherine of Alexandria following her death.

The monastery was built by Justinian and Theodora in 527. Today it is also famous for the Codex Siniaticus, a fourth century manuscript of the New Testament, which was discovered in 1844, and which plays a key role in Biblical scholarship today.

The monastery of Megaspilion, near Kalavrita, whose monks played a leading role in the War of Independence, is constructed entirely in the shelter of a huge cave in the side of a mountain. Its greatest treasure is a miraculous icon of the Mother of God attributed to Saint Luke, and discovered in the great cavern by a shepherdess, Euphrosyne, in 362. Unfortunately, the ancient buildings were largely destroyed in a huge fire in 1934 when a powder magazine dating from the War of Independence exploded.

Overlooking the town of Kalambaka tower the precipitous rocks of Meteora: isolated masses of rock rising sheer out of the flat valley-bottom. Inevitably, hermits sought refuge from danger there in troubled times. A monastery had been founded before 1336, soon to be followed by others, until by the time of Sulemein the Magnificent there were thirteen, together with some twenty smaller settlements. Some came to possess vast estates on the Danube in Wallachia (now Rumania).

The spectacularly sited monasteries are perched on the top of inaccessible cliffs, to which the only access used to be by ladders, which could be drawn up if necessary, or by winch and net. Some of the wooden ladders were over a hundred feet long. Alternatively, the ascent could be made in a net, hauled up on ropes from wind-lasses placed in specially constructed towers over-hanging the abyss. It was only in 1920 that steps were cut into the rock to allow easier access.

The monasteries of Meteora.

Below: Windlass still used to transport goods and people

Opposite page, bottom right: Ossuary

The fortunes of the monks of Meteora declined rapidly during the eighteenth century. Today many of the monasteries are in ruins. The area has become a tourist magnet, and the hordes of visitors have virtually driven away most of the remaining monks.

The Holy Mountain

The most famous centre of Orthodox monasticism is the monastic republic on the Holy Mountain of Athos, at the end of the northernmost of the three peninsulas which jut out into the Aegean Sea from Chalcis. This entire area is a colony of monasteries. There and now twenty, each of which has many more *kellia* and *sketai* under them, and hermits associated with them. All these *lavras* are *stauropegia*. No bishop but the Ecumenical Patriarch has any jurisdiction over them. The Holy Mountain falls under the ecclesiastical supervision of the ecumenical patriarchate and the secular protection of the Greek state.

Access to the monastic republic is limited to males. It is said that every time a Byzantine empress or princess tried to approach, she was turned back by the Virgin herself. Thus one monk who was brought to Athos as an orphan baby, and who died during the Second World War, never saw a human female in his life.

Each "day", that is, the period of daylight, is divided into twelve hours, and each "night", i.e. Period of darkness, into another twelve. Thus the "hours" of day are longer during the summer than during the winter; and the "hours" of night longer during the winter than during the summer. This is because the monks still follow Byzantine time, which preceded the invention of mechanical clocks, which for their useful functioning required that each hour be a fixed period of time of the same length. Thus the moment of sunset is counted as twelve o'clock, and the beginning of a new calendar day. Only the "trendy" monastery of Vatopedi has made the change to mechanical time.

The food available to the monks is plain, to say the least, and according to visitors, prepared without much regard for taste. Meat, fish and dairy products are avoided, together with olive oil, a staple of Greek cooking. On fast days there are further restrictions.

Saint Athanasios the Athonite

Inaccessible Athos had probably long been a haunt of hermits when large numbers of monks, driven out of their monasteries in Egypt and Syria by the Arab conquests, settled there in the seventh century. During the Iconoclastic Controversy of the early ninth century, when monks were persecuted by the Byzantine emperors more monks congregated there in large numbers.

After the persecutions had ended, the Emperor Basil issued a decree or *chrysobull* (c. 885) drew the boundaries of Mount Athos, and reserved it exclusively for the use of monks and hermits, forbidding outsiders, especially the Vlach shepherds who had pastured their animals on the mountain, to interfere with them. The *chrysobull* names the peninsula as the "garden of the Virgin", a reference to a legend that the Virgin Mary herself had once visited the mountain when her ship was carried there by a storm. Impressed by the natural beauty of the place, she asked her son to give it to her as a present, and a voice spoke from heaven saying: "Let this place be your garden and your inheritance; a haven and a paradise for those seeking salvation." The Byzantine Emperors who followed Basil pursued a

Above: The port of the monastery of Zografou
Below: The monastery of Xenofontos

similar policy solidifying from time to time the political autonomy of the community by further *chrysobulls*. From the ninth century to the fifteenth Athos enjoyed political independence. Even the emperors did not interfere, except only upon request from the monks.

The oldest surviving monastery, the Great Lavra, was founded in the tenth century by Saint Athanasius. Gradually others were founded round it. During the twelfth century monasteries were founded by Serbians, Russians, Georgians and Latins (Roman Catholics).

After the Fourth Crusade, when an attempt was made to force the Greeks to adopt Roman Catholic customs, many of the monasteries were plundered, and some of the monks were tortured and killed or expelled. The low point came when a band of Catalan mercenaries raided the mountain and destroyed many of the monasteries.

When the Turks approached in 1430, the submission of the monks to Murad II, more than thirty years before the fall of Constantinople, saved Athos from destruction and secured the preservation of the monks' political autonomy. The Turkish Sultans who succeeded the Byzantine Emperors on the throne of Constantinople seldom deviated from the policy of non-interference. In some ways, Athos enjoyed more freedom under the Turks than under the Byzantines, for the Sultans were less interested in the problems that arose within the community than the Byzantine emperors had been.

Turkish sovereignty came to an end in 1912, when the Greek fleet took possession of the Holy Mountain. A period of uncertainty as to the future status of the mountain followed, because Russia insisted that an international commission composed of all the Orthodox nations should assume control. Naturally, the Greek government did not agree, and the Russian revolution of 1917 brought that plan to an abrupt termination. By the Treaty of Lausanne (1923) Greece was granted the sovereignty over the monastic community.

In 1924, a committee composed of representatives of the Greek state and the Holy Community was appointed to draw up a constitution to determine relations between the monasteries and the Greek state. Since that time, all monks inhabiting Mount Athos are deemed to be Greek subjects, irrespective of their previous nationality. Justice is dispensed by the monastic authorities, but penal cases are referred to the civil courts at Thessaloniki. The representative of the Greek State on Athos executes, through those under his command, the decisions of the Holy Assembly and of the monasteries, provided, they are in accord with the constitution. The ecclesiastical authorities may call upon the forces of the state to enforce the appearance of a witness summoned to appear before an ecclesiastical court. In case a condemned person refuses to abide by the decision reached by the ecclesiastical courts, such decisions may be relayed to the civil authorities which are under the obligation to enforce it. The monks were exempted from military service and from much taxation, and their seas and forests from the normal regulations imposed by the Greek state.

At the beginning of the nineteenth century, half the monks on the Holy Mountain were non-Greek: Russians, Rumanians, Bulgarians, Serbs, etc. Then the revolutions of 1917 cut off the supply of recruits from Russia.

There has been considerable hostility to the monks within Greece. In 1926, the dictator Theodore Pangalos proposed turning Mount Athos into a casino. During the mid-1930s, the Greek sociologist Michael Choukas found that many monks "wrecks of a cruel world."

Above:The monastery of Docheiariou
Below:The monastery of Ay. Panteleimon (the Russian monastery)

"Some of them had found their wives deceiving them; others had lost their wealth in unsuccessful enterprises beyond recovery. To all of them, exile from normal social life appeared as the only escape from oppressive social circumstances."[2] According to the chief of police: "There are between fifty and sixty criminals on the mountain today who have disguised themselves as monks… We are doing all we can to find them and have them expelled, but unfortunately, we are not assisted in our task by the monastic authorities, because of their attitude that one of the functions of a Christian monastery is to give an opportunity to a sinner to repent, and their expectation that some of these criminals will ultimately join a monastery… Oh, there must be more than that number in the monasteries as fully-fledged monks."[3] Some of the monks averred that "Many monks come here to make money."[4] They accumulated wealth while working in idiorhythmic monasteries, and by receiving tips from visitors.

Choukas considered that the monks would be extinct in the next generation, if not sooner. For a long time, events seemed to show that although things were moving more slowly than he had anticipated, extinction was not far off. Following the Second World War, the occupation of much of Eastern Europe by the Red Army, and of Yugoslavia by the Communist partisans, together with the setting in of the Cold War, cut off recruits from Rumania, Bulgaria and Serbia.

During the 1970s, however, the tide turned. Kallistos Ware identified several factors as responsible: a reaction to the increasing secularisation of Greek life; the decay of semi-monastic brotherhoods, which had previously attracted many of those who would otherwise have gone to the Mountain, and the development of tourism to an extent which has made the religious life difficult in the more accessible monasteries, such as Meteora. However, additionally, he cites the positive inspirational influence of several charismatic abbots of unusual calibre.[5] Moreover, at the end of the twentieth century, with the collapse of Communism in Eastern Europe and the end of the Cold War, the northerners began to return from Serbia, Bulgaria, Romania and, above all, from Russia. Thus today the situation is looking healthier than for a long time.

During the long years of prayer and worship, many monks of Athos came to be recognised as saints in the Orthodox Church. The theologian Gregory Palamas became a great metropolitan of Thessaloniki. Saint Nephon, the saintly metropolitan of Thessaloniki and patriarch of Constantinople, went to evangelise the area which is now called Rumania. Saint Kosmas of Aitolia was a great preacher and educationalist before his martyrdom. Saint Savvas, from the skete of Anna, died on Kalymnos in 1948, where his body is said to exude a heavenly fragrance.

Many became martyrs, such as the abbot of Ivrion and thirteen monks who were bound, taken out to sea and drowned for refusing to adopt Catholic practices, and the twenty-four monks of Xeropotamou, burned alive in the tower of their monastery for the same reason. Patriarch Gregory V, executed by the Turks in reprisal for the Greek struggle for independence, was a monk of Athos.

Some were inevitably the subject of colourful legends. According to one such, the deacon Vimataris hid an icon of the Virgin in a well when barbarians raided the Vatopaidiou monastery, and was taken as a slave by them. He lived in captivity for seventy years before

The controversial monastery of Esfigmenou

he was freed. When he returned to his monastery on Mount Athos, it is said that the first thing that he saw was the icon standing upright on the water of the well with a large candle he had left there still burning after so many years.

The central village of Karyes is a strange one: a village without women and children, and where smoking, whistling and secular music are forbidden. There live the members of the *koinotis*, the governing assembly of the Holy Mountain, which meets twice a year. Its twenty members are chosen by election each year, one from each monastery. During the year of their election, these monks live in the central village of Karyes. For practical purposes, between meetings of the assembly, the holy Community is governed by a committee of four monks, the *epistasia*, made up of one fifth of the council. Each monastery is represented on the *epistasia* for one year in every five. One member of this committee, chosen from one of the five "senior monasteries" acts as their president, or *protoepistates*. A civil governor responsible to the Ministry of Foreign Affairs in Athens resides in Karyes. He heads a small company of administrators and policemen. In Karyes also is the church of the Protaton, dating from 967, is the central church of the entire community and the common property of all the monasteries. The port of Daphne, which serves the entire peninsula, has hotels, restaurants and post office, etc.

In recent years two problems have chiefly disturbed the peace of the Holy Mountain.

Some feminist Eurodeputies have challenged the legitimacy of the ban on women in territory which lies within the European Union, arguing that it is in breach of human rights legislation. However, in the treaty by which Greece was incorporated into the European

Community, the special status of the Holy Mountain was recognised and safeguarded.

A more dramatic problem has developed between the patriarchate and the one hundred or so monks of the Esfigmenou monastery. The latter, a fiercely conservative community, resented profoundly the opening of ecumenical dialogue between the patriarchate and the papacy. As a result, since 1972 they have refused to mention the patriarch in their prayers, or acknowledge the legitimacy of the *iera epistasia*. In December 2002 the patriarch and the Holy Synod of Constantinople declared the rebel monks to be in schism, and their community effectively defunct. In January 2003 the civil Governor of Mount Athos ordered them to vacate the monastery premises. When they refused to leave, police surrounded the monastery, and one of the monks died in an accident while trying to move a tractor across country during the night. At the time of going to press, this standoff continues.

The Angelic Life Today

Today the religious life is enjoying something of a revival. Religious houses tend to be rather small, but numerous: there are over eight hundred monasteries and their cells across the country. Nearly two hundred are to be found in the *nome*, or county, of Attica alone. Over eighty of these latter, however, belong to the Old Calendarists.[5] As in the Roman Catholic Church the balance between males and females altered in the twentieth century, with the previous overwhelming preponderance of males being replaced with a distinct preponderance of females.

One questionable aspect of the monastic life in Greece today is that many "monks" are attached to a monastery only nominally. Seeking advancement in the church as priests, they remain unmarried and for that reason find it necessary to become monks, but they live outside their monastery and are involved in parish work, especially in preaching. In this way they can make themselves well known to the higher authorities, and so become eligible for promotion to a bishopric. Thus, paradoxically, the monastic tonsure has become a stage in a recognised career track for the ambitious cleric.

Many of the hierarchy of the Greek Church at the present day, including the archbishop himself, were in this way loosely attached to a single monastic community nominally resident at Meteora, but since 1973 in Attica, and known as Chrysopigi, founded by Kallinikos, bishop of Piraeus, Ambrose, bishop of Kalavryta and Chrysostom, then bishop of Dimitriada (Volos) . This practice, in addition to creating divisions within the clergy between those on the "fast track" and those destined to remain parish priests for ever, sometimes raises the charge that many of the monasteries function chiefly as "hotels for the clergy."

8

The Faith Received from the Apostles

Authority in the Church

The Orthodox Church sees its faith as something received from Holy Tradition. Prominent in this tradition are the holy Scriptures, the Nicene Creed, the dogmatic formulations of the Seven Great Councils of the Church, the writings of the Church fathers and the holy Liturgy. Orthodox theologians feel that the Roman Catholic Church has distorted the original Christian faith by adding to it, whereas Protestant denominations have gone astray by deleting essential doctrines.

The various books which make up the New Testament were created within the early Christian communities. It was those communities acting collectively in a synod at Laodicea in 367, which decided which books could be regarded as authoritative, in that they taught the faith received from the apostles, and which were spurious. For the Orthodox, aware as they are of the origins of the Scriptures, they derive their authority from the Church in which they were produced, and cannot be set in artificial isolation above it, as Protestants tend to do; as though they had come straight from God, independently of any particular social, cultural or historical circumstances. Moreover, according to the Orthodox, it is the Church alone, from which the Scriptures emerged, which can interpret them authoritatively.The supreme authority in the Church is an ecumenical council, an assembly of the bishops of all the Orthodox Churches which has the authority to determine all questions of doctrine and church law. Seven have been recognised. These have produced definitive statements of faith, the Creeds, which express the common Christian faith. The formulations of the Seven Ecumenical Councils of the Church also carry the ultimate authority of the whole Church. Of these pronouncements, the chief general guide to the faith is the Nicene Creed, recited during the liturgy and at the office of compline. In addition to the formulations of the Seven Ecumenical Councils, the decisions of local councils and statements of faith made by local councils and individual bishops also have authority, although they cannot be treated as final, since they are liable to error. Thus two works written in the seventeenth century as a defence against Protestant tendencies within the Orthodox Church are sometimes considered as minor standards of faith: the *Confessio Orthodoxa* of 1638 of Peter Mogila, Metropolitan of Kiev, and the *Confessio Dosithei* of 1672 of Dositheus.

Another source of faith is the writings of the "Fathers of the Church", theologians whose works have received general acceptance and respect within the Church. Again, these individuals may have erred at particular times, and have to be read intelligently and with discrimination. Moreover, there is no definite list of "approved" Fathers, and some would include those whom others would exclude, but there is general consensus about most, such as Gregory of Nazianzus, Basil the Great and John Chrysostom.

In addition, much of the faith of the Church is transmitted in its worship: in the liturgy and offices and in the performance of its sacramental rituals.

This understanding of authority is more complex, and much more sophisticated, than that of those Roman Catholics who ascribe all final authority to the pronouncements of the Popes alone, and to those Protestants who regard Scripture, sometimes as literally and naively understood, as the only ultimate authority for Christians. Nor does it have the emptiness of that standard of faith sometimes appealed to by Anglicans: "What has been believed by everyone, everywhere and at all times."

In content, the faith of the Orthodox Church is identical in almost all matters of substance with that of the Roman Catholics, particularly since the reforms of the Second Vatican Council. The foundations of the Orthodox faith are belief in one God in three Persons, in the Incarnation of God the Son, in his redeeming death and resurrection, and in the Church founded by him with its Sacraments, and in life after death. It has been stated that the Greek Orthodox Christian lives in much the same religious atmosphere do the Roman Catholics of Southern Europe, and his Church stands in every way nearer to the Roman Catholic Church than any other religious body.

In order not to repeat what is already well-known to readers, only the differences between the Orthodox and Catholics will be noted here, although in doing so it is necessary to stress the point that merely by singling them out for treatment, these differences are likely thereby to be exaggerated. A list of differences is inherently liable to induce a distorted sense of proportion. The Catholic writer Adrian Fortescue, however, has pointed out that "It is in the points about which Protestants disagree that we see how near the Orthodox Church is to us."[1] The chief significant points of difference with Catholics are the *flilioque* clause in the creed, the moment of consecration of the bread and wine in the Liturgy, Purgatory, and the Primacy of the Roman Pope.

For the Orthodox, the faith comes from, and is based upon, tradition. In practice, the most important norm of traditional Orthodox doctrine is the Liturgy. In particular, the Nicene Creed, formulated in ecumenical councils and used during every celebration of the Liturgy, is particularly important. When Western Christians added the clause "and the Son" to this statement of faith, it was a cause of considerable outrage and scandal in the East.

The addition was first introduced in the sixth century somewhere in Spain. The contemporary Orthodox theologian, Nicolas Zernov, concedes that the bishops who originally made the change probably acted with the best intentions, and that they had no desire to amend a creed which had been the uniting link for the whole Church, but were desirous merely to combat the views of certain Arian heretics in that country who denied the full divinity of Jesus. By inserting the *Filioque* clause the Spanish bishops were trying to give an additional proof of the complete equality of the Father and the Son, and therefore they described the Holy Spirit as proceeding from both. He concedes that until this matter became controversial, theologians frequently wrote about the Holy Spirit as coming from the Father through the Son, or from the Father and the Son. No one had considered that such expressions implied heresy, as no one questioned the text of the creed.

Some Orthodox theologians nevertheless argue that the *filioque* gives "dogmatic authority to an incorrect concept of the Trinity."[3] The arguments raised by Photius had been that "the *Filioque* is an illegitimate interpolation," which presupposed a confusion of the hypostatic characters of the Persons of the Trinity, "destroys the *monarchy* of the Father" and "relativises the reality of personal, or hypostatic existence, in the Trinity." "In his encyclical to the Eastern patriarchs (866), Photius described the introduced of the *Filioque* by the Frankish missionaries in Bulgaria as the "crown of evils"."[4] Peter, Patriarch of Antioch, who objected to the systematic anti-Latinism of his colleague in Constantinople, Michael Cerularius, considered the interpolation as an "evil, and even the worst of evils." Other Orthodox theologians complain of the complete futility of the endless controversy which the dispute has generated. Byzantine literature on the subject of the *Filioque* clause is voluminous. The debate was frequently reduced to an interminable enumeration by both sides of patristic texts collected in favour of the respective positions of each party However, Nicolas Zernov points out that the very fact that a local Church dared to alter an Ecumenical creed solemnly approved by the whole of Christendom showed a serious defect in their conception of the Church. Once the West accepted the *Filioque* clause against the wishes of the East, affirming that it was fully justified in so doing, it repudiated the unity of the Church.

Roman Catholics regard the words by which Jesus instituted the sacrament of Communion: "Take, eat, this is my Body..." and "Take, drink of this, for this is my Blood..." as effecting a change in the bread and wine into the body and blood of Christ. The Orthodox likewise believe in the divine presence in the consecrated bread and wine in the Eucharist, but they are less inclined to seek a single moment of transformation. The Liturgy invokes the Holy Spirit to change the bread and wine into the Body and Blood of Christ, but does so *after* the words of Institution when he prays that God will: "be graciously pleased that Your Holy Spirit may come down upon us and upon these gifts set forth, to bless, and hallow ... and make this bread the precious Body of your Christ, and what is in this cup the precious Blood of your Christ, changing them by your Holy Spirit."

The Orthodox and Catholic paths diverged before the full development in the West of the idea of Purgatory. The Orthodox believe that after death a provisional judgement is passed upon the soul, which enters into an intermediate state, to await the return of Christ and the Final Judgement. The saints are believed to go straight to Heaven, where they enter the presence of God. They do not, however, attain final beatitude until the entrance into eternal life of all who have attained salvation. Unlike the Western Church, there was no development of ideas about the nature of this intermediate state, and no practice of the purchase of indulgences to relieve suffering there, although praying for the dead is frequently practised.

Of all the differences, in practice it is the Catholic's belief in the primacy of the Roman Patriarch over all the others, which was later developed into the dogma of papal infallibility, which is most divisive. The replacement of the collegiate authority of the bishops of the Church by a centralist monarchical system is held by the Orthodox to be a novelty which is contrary to the tradition the Church has received from the apostles.

The Orthodox Viewpoint

Despite the small number of real theological differences between Orthodox and Catholics, there are many areas of significant differences of thought and perspective. As Peter Hammond points out "the manifest cleavage which now exists between the Orthodox and other Christians is less a matter of disagreement on specific issues than of two widely divergent attitudes and approaches."[3]

It has been observed that Orthodox Christology focuses the union of two natures in the one person, without giving much attention to the particularities of the historical person of Jesus. In practice, the divine nature of Christ overshadows His humanity. This is evident in the passages from the Church's hymnology already quoted above.

The Orthodox seem to be more consistently aware than Western Christians of the spiritual world of angels, which is often mentioned in the Liturgy. These invisible creatures stand before the throne of God in worship, but they are also thought of as agents of God, who intercede in Heaven, and serve as the guardians of mankind on earth.

Man is seen as the "connecting link between visible and invisible nature." He was created perfect, destined for the contemplation of God, and endowed with incorruptibility and immortality. After the Fall, Man lost these supernatural qualities but retained free will and the power to do good, in both cases to a diminished degree. The image of God in which he was created was marred, but not obliterated. The Orthodox place little emphasis upon the difficult Western idea of original sin. Death and transitoriness have been handed on from Adam to all his descendents, but Orthodoxy does not regard the guilt associated with sin as transmissible.

The Orthodox believe that through His Resurrection, Christ restored our original incorruptibility, and deified human nature. Salvation is not merely a matter of rescue from sin, but also from the power of evil as manifest in the fact of death. Salvation is understood primarily as victory over death, and the deification of humanity. Thus the Redemption brought by Christ is connected by the Orthodox not only with His Crucifixion, but more especially with His Resurrection. In no other Church is belief in the Resurrection so dominant, not only in theology, but in the language of its worship as well.

Unlike the West, the Orthodox Church has developed no detailed doctrine of Grace. Western theologians were compelled to give considerable attention to the relationship between the Grace of God and human free will by the Pelagian controversy in the fifth century, while the Eastern Church was hardly affected by this dispute. The Orthodox hold that man is free to accept or to reject God's offer of mercy. If that offer is accepted, then human effort and God's Grace cooperate together. Man is said to be justified by faith and works, and not by faith alone.

The Virgin Mary occupies a prominent place both in theology and in the devotional life. She is the "Mother of God" (*Theotokos*), and ever-Virgin. The Liturgy is full of the praise of Mary, and her name occurs almost as frequently as that of Jesus. Several times during the course of the liturgy she is referred to as "our most holy, most pure, most blessed and glorious Lady, the Mother of God and ever-virgin Mary." In ordinary speech she is the *Panayia* or "all-holy One", or the *Megalochari*, "the One who is full of grace". However, Orthodoxy has no doctrine of her Immaculate Conception, since this depends upon the

*Icon of the
Falling Asleep
of the Virgin
(Byzantine
Museum, Athens)*

concept of original sin, which did not develop in the East. A few Orthodox theologians have even asserted that Mary was not entirely free from sin, since sinlessness is an attribute which properly belongs to Christ alone.

With the exception of saints and martyrs, all souls pass after death to Hades, where they have a foretaste either of eternal life or of eternal damnation. At the Last Judgement, the bodies of all men will be raised and united with their souls. The bodies of the saved are transfigured like the body of Christ on the Mount of Tabor, and their souls behold the Holy Trinity. This concept of the deification of man, a development of eschatology peculiar to the Orthodox Church, is compared to the heating of iron in fire. As the heat permeates the iron, it becomes transformed, yet without ceasing remain iron. Similarly man will become divine, without ceasing to be human.

105

*Veneration of the Gifts of the Magi in a reliquary
in the Church of Nea Ionia, in the suburbs of Athens
The relics were brought from Mount Athos*

The Orthodox Church invokes the saints and prays for their intercession, and like the Roman Catholics, Orthodox venerate their material remains, or relics, which are said already to share in the glory of the future state of mankind.

By contrast, the damned will be delivered to the everlasting fire. However, a number of Orthodox theologians reject the doctrine of Eternal Punishment as incompatible with the goodness and omnipotence of God.

Part Two

Icon of Saint George - 18th century
(Byzantine Museum, Athens)

9

The Great Synthesis

The account of the origins of Greek Christianity is one with the beginnings of Christianity itself. Initially, the new religion was seen by contemporaries as an outgrowth of Judaism, and by the Jews themselves as a Jewish heresy. Some of the first Christians believed that they should carry out their mission only to fellow Jews, and that they should observe all the religious laws and customs of the Jews in their entirety. This issue came to a head when the leaders of the Church gathered together in council in Jerusalem. After lengthy deliberations they issued their unanimous decision, prefaced with the words "It seemed good to the Holy Spirit and to us…", in favour not requiring converts to Christianity to conform to the Jewish Law, and of launching a mission to the Gentiles. The defeated "Judaisers", a rump centred upon Jerusalem, died out altogether after the destruction of that city by the Romans in AD 70, following a revolt.

At this period, the people who called themselves Hellenes were spread across the ancient world. Colonisation movements of the eighth century BC had taken them from the Greek peninsula to the coasts of what is now Italy, France and Spain in the west, to the shores of North Africa in the south, to the coasts of Thrace in the north, and in much larger numbers to the littoral of Asia Minor and the far reaches of the Black Sea in the east. The Greek cities which flourished along the Asian shores, such as Miletus and Smyrna, had given birth to philosophical and scientific thought. Subsequently, Greeks and Greek culture quickly spread across the Near East with the conquests of Alexander the Great; and his successors ruled from the deserts of Libya to the borders of India. The language of the educated in Asia Minor, Syria and Egypt became Greek. The Ptolemaic pharaohs of Egypt, of whom Cleopatra was the most famous and the last, were Greeks. In the great library of Alexandria, the literature of the ancient world was translated into Greek and stored for the use of research scholars. Among these ancient works was the Septuagint, a Greek translation of the Hebrew scriptures. By the time of Christ, when people of one culture wanted to communicate with those of another, they would usually do so in Greek. Consequently, the gospels and other religious books of the New Testament were first written in the Greek language.[1] The word "Christ" is itself a Greek word.

The Graeco-Roman world had by that time already moved away from the simple, unreflective paganism of the classical period. Relative ease of communication and travel since the time of Alexander had made impossible, for an educated man, a naïve belief in the gods of one's own people and ignorance of, or rejection of, all others. This had led at first to a process of "borrowing". A cosmopolitan port, like Piraeus, acquired many temples of foreign gods, such as Egyptian Isis; while non-Greek Roman emperors came Eleusis to be initiated into the Greek Mysteries. The next step was the process called syncretism, the identification of one's own gods with those of other peoples: "The god we Greeks call Zeus, you Romans call Jupiter," etc. But among the intellectuals since the time of Plato there had been a tendency towards monotheism. This was to develop slowly but steadily, and was to reach its fullest and most definitive philosophical expression in the work of Plotinus at the beginning of the third century AD.

At the same time, another version of monotheism, that of the "jealous God" of the Jews, whose main actions in history seem to have been unaccountably to favour one "chosen" people over all the rest, was being transported to the cities of the Roman world by the Jewish Diaspora. While this "tribal" version of monotheism was welcomed by a few, its arrogant self-righteousness and exclusivity was generally regarded as both irrational and antisocial in the ancient world. The religion we know as Christianity was to emerge as the result of a synthesis between these two forms of monotheism, the teaching of the Jewish Jesus as transmitted in the writings of the evangelists and the apostle Paul, and philosophical ideas current at that time in the Greek intellectual world. Unfortunately, the Jewish element in the mix, with its tendency to intellectual absolutism, moral self-righteousness, and puritan hang-ups, were to generate unpleasant aspects of Christianity.

The origins of this synthesis lie in the work and writings of the apostle Paul. Paul and Barnabas were ordained by the elders of the Church at Antioch to work as missionaries in the Greek world. They began at Salamis, in Cyprus, legendary birthplace of goddess Aphrodite. There Paul's understanding passed beyond the narrow and bigoted outlook of Judaism, teaching that Christ was a Saviour for all mankind, and not merely of a chosen few. He argued that regardless of racial ancestry and religious observance, everyone, whether Jew or Gentile, could please God, and could do so without the need to conform to the Jewish legal system. On the basis of this single insight, the strict monotheism of Judaism was able to draw upon the tolerant universalist tradition of philosophical monotheism developing in the contemporary world, and so, in time, gain access to all the intellectual tools available in the Roman world: concepts developed in the Greek language and embodied in Platonic metaphysics, Aristotelian logic, and Stoic ethics.

After his mission to Cyprus Paul returned to the mainland and, using the network of Hellenised Diaspora Jews, carried the Christian Gospel throughout the Greek cities of Asia Minor. Then, while staying at Troas, he believed that he received a vision of a man of Macedonia, inviting him to cross the narrow straits to Europe.

Soon afterwards, Paul made the sea crossing, and landed at Neapolis (now Kavalla) the port which served Philippi, the provincial capital and a garrison town. There, he established the first Christian community in Europe. Loukas and Lydia, two of the most prominent citizens, became his first converts. After exorcising a slave girl, he was thrown into prison, from which he was supposedly delivered miraculously when the prison doors opened of their own accord during an earthquake, and the jailer and his family were converted.

Paul then moved on to Thessaloniki. At that time the capital of the region and the largest port in the Aegean, it was connected both to Rome and Byzantium, and the trade

Early altars (Byzantine Museum, Athens)

route to Asia, by way of the Via Egnatia. It was thus a great political and commercial centre, with communications with the rest of the empire by land and sea. There Paul established a Church of both Jewish and Greek converts. After some were imprisoned, Paul escaped by night to Veria, where his preaching in the synagogue was more readily received.

After that, he went to Athens by sea. There, according to local tradition, he landed in Glyfada, and as he travelled through the district now known as Nea Smyrni, passed an altar dedicated to "the unknown gods", which he was later to refer to in his preaching. On entering this city, which was the crown and centre of Hellenic culture, he preached his famous sermon on the "Unknown God" on the Areopagos Hill, below the Acropolis. The Athenians listened patiently until Paul spoke of Christ's resurrection from the dead, at which point they decided that he was a charlatan.

After Athens Paul settled for some time in Corinth, a city noted for its commercial prosperity and as a centre of the worship of Aphrodite, famous for its slave markets and sacred brothels. Paul remained in Corinth for a year and a half, setting up another Christian community, before returning to Asia..

This mission among the Greeks was so effective that Paul has been called the apostle of Greece, and a second founder of Christianity. Saint Paul later returned to Corinth twice and to Macedonia once. Finally, late in the year 61, on his way to face trial in Rome, he briefly landed on the southern coast of Crete, at Kali Limenes.

Tradition also ascribes missionary work in Greece to other apostles and evangelists and their immediate successors. Saint Luke is said to have visited various parts of the country. The apostle Philip was believed to have stayed in Athens. Saint John received his apocalyptic visions on Patmos, and later settled on the nearby Asian shore in the Greek city of Ephesus with the ageing Virgin Mary. Tradition has it that Saint Andrew was martyred in

Patras. Titus, a disciple of Paul, evangelised the island of Crete. Thus "...the early Christian movement was given birth, nourishment and astonishing development in Greek surroundings. The Christian communities recorded their first triumphs against paganism in numerous Greek cities... The Church by and large, grew upon Greek soil with the life of the city-states exerting a profound and lasting influence upon the development of Christianity."[3] It was in Greece that Christianity was able to evolve into a universal religious movement.

Among the Greeks metaphysical speculation was natural, thus Greek Christians welcomed the light of reason with which to elucidate the ideas they proclaimed. To do this, Greece gave the new religion its language, and the forms of thought into which the spirit and meaning of its philosophy could be rendered. The subtlety of this language, combined with its widespread currency in the ancient world, endowed it as a peculiarly appropriate medium for the dissemination of the new religion. Historian Arthur Toynbee points out: "A language is not an emotionally and intellectually neutral means of communication. Every language conveys a distinctive way of feeling and thinking, and the Attic *koine* made its own impress on the Jewish scriptures when these were translated into it, and on the constituents of the Christian *New Testament* when these were composed in the *koine* itself. The Epistles attributed to Saint Paul ... and the Gospel according to Saint John contain theological passages which could not have been written without some acquaintance with the Hellenic Greek philosophical vocabulary and without some grasp of the meaning of its terms."[4] As the apologists of Christianity used the concepts readily available in Greek philosophy to explain their message, and as educated people increasingly began to try to "make sense" out of it in the intellectual terms of their day, the insights of the followers of Plato, Aristotle, and the Stoics penetrated into the very heart of Christian thought. In consequence, Toynbee observes: "...in all of Christianity's subsequent differentiations, there is an indelible Greek, as well as Jewish, element."[5] It would not be an exaggeration to say that during this early stage of its development, Christianity became Hellenised.

Clement of Alexandria, an Athenian-born convert of the late second century, and others came to regard the philosophy of Greece as a preparation for the Christian Gospel, parallel to that of the teachings of the Hebrew prophets and the Mosaic Law. Platonic and Neoplatonic philosophy and the ethical principles of Stoicism became an integral part of Christian thought. In time, Plato and Aristotle were to became the dominant influences in a new, and genuinely Christian, philosophy.

Of course, every movement generates its own opposition; and there were always some, like Justin Martyr, who demanded to know: "What does Athens have to do with Jerusalem, the Academy with the Church?" Despite the predominance of the Hellenising movement, there would always be two strands within Christianity: one rational, universalist and tolerant, stemming from its Hellenic base; and the other, irrational, rigid, legalistic, dogmatic and intolerant, a throwback to its Jewish origins. Sometimes one strand would predominate, and sometimes the other.

In the beginning, even the Church in the city of Rome was a Greek Church: "a colony ... of Greek Christians and Graecized Jews."[6] The first churches of the West were originally Greek: "their language was Greek, their organisation Greek, their writers Greek their scriptures Greek, and many traditions show that their liturgy was Greek."[7]

Left: Christ as Orpheus (Byzantine Museum, Athens)

Right: Christian symbols (Byzantine Museum, Athens)

Nor was it merely in its thought, but also in its organisation that the Church, as its numbers grew, became thoroughly Hellenised. While models of organisation were found in the Roman civil administration, it was under the influence of the Greek mystery religions, with their period of preparation and instruction prior to initiation, subsequently called in the Church the catechumenate, and their solemn rites of initiation, that its sacramental and liturgical tradition developed.

With the need for the emperor Nero to find a scapegoat for the burning of Rome in 64, the already unpopular Christians were blamed for the disaster, and a long period of sporadic persecution began. The martyrs which these generated become the object of a cult within the Church, although the Christian theologian Origen struck a dissonant note when he admitted: "Those who have died for the Christian faith at different times have been few and are easily counted."[8] Despite the persecutions, and the strong rivalry of other religious movements, such as Manicheanism for the hearts and minds of the peoples of the Empire, by the fourth century the Christian Church had become the most influential popular institution in the world.

10

The Realm of Light

The Church Triumphant

The reign of the emperor Constantine the Great (292-337) was fundamental to the development of the entire Church, but especially for the Greeks, in two ways. Firstly, after winning a victory which gave him mastery of Rome, by the Edict of Milan of 313 Christianity became officially "tolerated." Constantine then adopted Christianity as the official religion of the empire.[1] He immediately began erecting churches, adding the bishops to the imperial payroll, and exempting the Christian clergy from civil duties. All but a very few Emperors from that time onwards supported Christianity at great public expense, and the Church became an integral part of the Imperial establishment.

Although Constantine's conversion was open to interpretation as a cynical political ploy, he nevertheless projected himself as "bishop of the Church to the world at large,"[1] and in return was extravagantly lauded by the bishops as "the equal of an apostle". Subsequent emperors inherited his position within the Church as a "sacred person". Emperors could preach sermons and received Holy Communion in the manner of a priest. On certain special occasions they would assist at the altar.

Constantine was soon to discover, however, that the adoption and patronage of Christianity did not ensure that religious divisions ceased to be a political problem, for it allowed disagreements among Christians which had hitherto seethed in secret to burst out into the open. With the emergence of the Church from the shadows of society into the full glare of public life, fundamental differences began to emerge over doctrine.

These disagreements generated heated controversies in which the mass of the newly-converted population enthusiastically took part in a way unimaginable to us today. A witness, Gregory of Nyssa, described the feverish atmosphere of the times thus: "The whole city is full of it, the squares, the market places, the crossroads, the alleyways; old-clothes men, money-changers, food-sellers: they are all busy arguing. If you ask someone to give you change, he philosophises about the Begotten and the Unbegotten; if you enquire about the price of a loaf, you are told by way of reply that the Father is greater and the Son inferior; if you ask 'Is my bath ready?' the attendant answers that the Son was made out of nothing." Since the Church was now such a widespread and popular institution, any major dispute within it carried severe consequences for the unity of the empire itself. Constantine consequently saw it as his duty to intervene in any theological dispute in order to secure a settlement which could carry as near universal assent as possible.

In order to settle a major dispute, about the nature of Christ, he summoned all the bishops of the Church together at Nicaea. The ecumenical council of Nicaea (325) condemned Arianism, the belief that Jesus is not truly God, but a created Demiurge or agent of God, something between the divine and the human. Over time, the Arians were reconciled to the Church, although the Goths in the West remained attached to their heresy for several centuries. This Council not only finally settled the dispute, as far as the empire was concerned, its work established the formula which was to be employed for the solution of all future controversies. The bishops would conduct their disputes in formal conference; afterwards, the losers would be condemned as heretics and punished by the state. Thus with remarkable speed, the persecuted became persecutors.

Another development during the reign of Constantine laid the seed for future division among Christians. Realising that the empire was too big to be governed from one central location, he divided it into two parts, one in the west to be ruled from Rome, and another in the east to be governed from a New Rome on the Bosporus. This strategic move found support from tradition, for most Romans believed, on the basis of no good evidence whatsoever, that they were descendants of the ancient Trojans, and that one day it would be their fortune to return to Ilium. The exact site chosen, Byzantium, an ancient colony of the Megarians, was transformed into a magnificent new imperial centre. In time, it would become known as the city of Constantine – Constantinople. On May 11th 330, the new capital was solemnly inaugurated, and the emperor and his government took up residence there. This development laid the seeds for a long process by which Eastern and Western Christians would grow apart.

The first sign of this occurred almost immediately, when Pope Damasus (366-384) commissioned a Latin edition of the Bible (the Vulgate). For some time the Roman Church had been losing its Hellenic character, and the use of Latin had been growing.

Early Christians recognised four churches of apostolic origin as having a leading position in the universal Church: Rome, Antioch, Alexandria and Jerusalem. The bishops of these sees were dignified by the title "patriarch". When Constantine chose his new capital, the see of Byzantium had been a minor bishopric under the metropolitan of Heraclea, a position clearly unsuitable for the bishop of New Rome. At the second ecumenical council, held in Constantinople in 381, this see was elevated to the rank of a patriarchate, and reckoned second only to that of Rome. Ominously for the future unity of the Church, old Rome refused to recognise the appearance of a new rival.

Controversies and Politics

The third ecumenical council, that of Ephesus (431), condemned Nestorius, who taught that Jesus was a man into whom the spirit of God had entered, and that Mary could not be called the Mother of God, only the mother of the man, Jesus. The Nestorians, most of whom lived beyond the boundaries of the empire in Mesopotamia, refused to accept the findings of the council, and their descendants, mostly living in Iraq, remain unreconciled today. For some time the Nestorian Church flourished, since they seemed more inclined to engage in evangelism than the Orthodox, and their missionaries reached as far as China; but their success proved ephemeral.

The fourth ecumenical council, held at Chalcedon (451), insisted that Christ had two natures, one divine and one human, against the Alexandrians, who held that he had only one indivisible nature. The so-called Monophysites were condemned. But these made up much of the population of Egypt and Syria within the empire, and Armenia beyond. The controversy was partly theological, but also partly political. It was in part a struggle for precedence between the patriarchates of Alexandria and Constantinople, and an expression of Egyptian and Syrian resistance to imperial hegemony. It drove a wedge between the Syrian, Egyptian and Armenian Churches, on the one hand, and the Byzantine and Latin on the other, creating resentment and enmity.

In 628 an Arab emissary confronted the emperor Heraclius in Jerusalem and presented him with a letter from "Mohammed, the messenger of God" demanding he renounce his faith and submit to Allah. When the Arabs swarmed out of their desert peninsula a few years later, very discontented and rebellious provinces of the empire lay before them, and they were easily able to sever the lands of the ancient patriarchates of Jerusalem, Antioch and Alexandria from the rest of the Church. By 642 the Persian empire had fallen, and by 695 North Africa was lost. How profound the isolation of those areas which fell under Arab control from the rest of Christendom was is revealed by an eleventh century Christian of Antioch, who explained that the name of no bishop of Rome was known to the Church there after Pope Agatho, who died in 681.[2] Pressure was put on the inhabitants of those lands to become Moslems, and over the centuries most were to convert. These conquests reduced the area of the once great Eastern Roman Empire to little more than Anatolia, the Aegean and the Balkans.

Paradoxically, neither the conversion of Constantine nor the imposition of Orthodoxy upon Christians had ensured the disappearance of paganism in Greece, but later emperors did their best to make the "Christian empire" a reality. Theodosius, known as "the Great" by a grateful Church, forbade any worshipper to enter a pagan temple, and put sacrifice to pagan gods on the same level as treason to the state. In 416 Theodosius II dismissed all pagans from the civil service and army. In 529 Justinian closed down the University of Athens. Meanwhile in the rural areas, the countrymen, or *pagani*, continued much as before, tolerantly grafting the new religion onto their existing folk beliefs, customary practices and festivals, which in northern areas of Greece seem to have centred upon the cult of Dionysos, and further south upon the veneration of Pan, and the nymphs who inhabited caves, streams and springs.

The Struggle over Images

The eighth century saw renewed and bitter controversy over the veneration of images, which threatened to rend the Church in the East. In 717 the army raised to the imperial throne Leo III, the Isaurian, an ill-educated, dogmatic puritan. Everything he did not understand or approve of, he denounced as superstition. He distrusted the Academy of the Sciences, so that building was set on fire, and thirteen distinguished professors, their students, and the library, were all consumed in the flames. He particularly abhorred the veneration of icons as idolatry, so the walls of the churches of Constantinople were repainted, first with vegetation and then with hunting scenes. Monasticism, he detested,

*Above: early ambo
(Byzantine Museum)
Above right: early sanctuary
(Byzantine Museum)*

since monks and nuns produced no soldiers. Thousands were driven into the arena and given the choice between immediate marriage, or blinding and exile. These changes found favour with many of the bishops, jealous of the popularity of the monks with the people, and a synod duly declared the painting and veneration of images to be idolatrous. There followed a long period of official persecution of the venerators of images by a succession of Isaurian emperors, known as the iconoclasts.

Women, in particular, resisted these changes. When a soldier removed the miraculous image of Christ from the Bronze Gate of the Hall of Audience of the Imperial palace, a crowd of enraged women knocked him off his ladder and beat him to death with clubs. It was noted without surprise among the people that a series of plagues and earthquakes followed the banning of images, and perhaps with some satisfaction, that the iconoclastic emperors suffered peculiarly horrifying deaths.

Constantine "Copronymus" (his real name is unknown, since monastic chroniclers changed it everywhere to "Name of Shit") chose an Athenian girl as wife for his son, Leo. The Athenians were devout image-worshippers, and Irene was able to assume control of the empire in her son's name when her husband died prematurely. Working very cautiously, she secured a council at Nicea which, in 787, restored the veneration of images. This was for a time in danger from her son, who ascended the imperial throne as Constantine VI. However, unpopular and incompetent, he was blinded and imprisoned in the Sacred Palace, to die later in obscurity, while his mother reigned in his stead. In her turn she fell victim to a palace coup, and forty years renewed persecution at the hands of a short succession of iconclasts followed. But once again, the women of the imperial family secured the iconoclasts' downfall. When the emperor Theophilus died, his consort, Theodora, opened the prisons and restored the icons. Throughout the night of February 19th 843, a doxology was chanted at the shrine of the Virgin at Blachernae, and then the people marched with lighted candles to complete their thanksgiving in the great church of Agia Sophia. Since that time, the veneration of icons has been unopposed in the Orthodox Church.

The triumph of the images led to a resurgence of religious vitality. First, Slavic peoples who had settled in Greece were converted, then in 860, two brothers from Thessaloniki, Cyril and Methodius, set out on missionary expeditions to the north. The effort they initiated was to be crowned, many years later, with the conversion of Russia.

The Realm of Light

With the end of the imperial succession in Rome, the empire had a single head ruling from a single capital. Although it is frequently known as the Byzantine Empire, it was essentially the Roman Empire, coterminous with the civilised world, controlled from a new Greek centre. But it was a baptised Roman Empire, ruled over by an emperor who, anointed and crowned, was thought of as the image on earth of Christ, the Lord of Creation. Thus the empire became the realm of Light not merely because of the brightness of ancient learning and culture, but also because it was illumined by the light of the true faith, and the place in which divine grace was showered down on earth through the working of the sacraments.

The emperor, the Lord of the World, the image and representative of God on earth, dwelt in the "Sacred Palace". His wealth was stored in the "Sacred Treasury", and his horses in the "Sacred Stables". He took part day by day in the liturgical observances of the Church, visiting orphans on the first day of Lent, washing the feet of twelve poor old men on Great Thursday, and so on. His Christlike nature was most vividly expressed at Easter, when: "Clad in white cerements, attended by the 'Twelve Apostles', he, having vanquished death and been resurrected, moved solemnly, amid roses and accompanied by the song of nightingales, through the garden of a honey-golden nature, which, like himself, had once again awakened to life."[8] On that day alone, all were equal and none need prostrate themselves before the imperial presence.

The commander of the Legions was now the warrior of Christ, and his every campaign by definition a crusade, or sacred war. The triumphant hymn of praise chanted upon his victorious return to the City expressed this in appropriate terms:

"Hail to You, Great King, the Ever-victorious, Beloved of God, Guided by God, Safeguarded by God. Long Life to him whose arm sustains the balance of the world. Son of God, preserve him. Son of God, enlighten him. Son of God, rule With him. Exalt the Christian Faith. Increase the courage of God's People. Through the mouth of the Successor of the Apostles, your city, Great King, proclaims you a second David, wise Hero of the Faith and Bulwark of Christendom."[9]

The bishops of the Council of Chalcedon called addressed the emperor as the "Teacher of the Faith." In 730 the emperor Leo wrote to Pope Gregory II: "Know, O Pope, that I am emperor and Pope combined into one."[10] This was inevitably to lead to conflict with the increasingly ambitious claims of the patriarchs of Rome, at this time effectively beyond the reach of imperial authority.

The Great Schism

Of all the controversies which beset the Church, the one which most concerns modern Christians is the split between the Eastern Christians under Constantinople, now called Orthodox, and the Western Christians who looked to Rome, now called Catholics. Relations between the two patriarchates continually bedevilled the Church during the centuries following the Constantinian settlement, a state of affairs which Sir Steven Runciman attributed to "the jealousy of the old for the newer capital."[3] In retaliation against increasingly ambitious Roman claims, in 595, the Patriarch John the Faster assumed the title "Ecumenical Patriarch", but this only further provoked Roman rivalry.

In the days before Constantine, when Rome had been the undisputed capital of the world, it was natural to regard it as the most suitable site to function as the religious capital, outranking all the other great cities of the empire, such as Alexandria and Antioch. The barbarian invasions of Italy, however, sidelined Rome and the Roman see. At the same time, they removed effective imperial control, leaving the bishops of Rome to develop their own ideas of Papal monarchy in comparative isolation. In time, knowledge of Greek died out in Italy, while that of Latin faded in Constantinople. The emperor Michael III was to call Latin a "barbarian and Scythian tongue."[4] Moreover, in a world where travel became increasingly difficult, the traditions of the two churches slowly began to evolve in different ways, rather in the manner in which the distinct dialects of a language may increasingly diverge, and may in time may become separate and mutually incomprehensible languages.

Despite these centrifugal tendencies, the sudden irruption of Islam, submerging the three ancient patriarchal sees of Antioch, Alexandria and Jerusalem, seems for a time to have brought Rome and Constantinople together. R. W. Southern has calculated that between 654 and 752, eleven popes had a mainly Greek background, and only six a mainly Latin one. This contrasts with the century before, when thirteen out of fifteen were Italians.[5] In 663 the emperor was received in Rome, and in

The conversion of the Bulgars, from the Chronicle of Constantine Manasi

119

710 the Pope in Constantinople. In 680 a council was held in Constantinople, to which the Pope sent delegates, at which all those present agreed in condemning as heretical four patriarchs of Constantinople and one Roman pope.

When the tide of Islam showed signs of having reached its zenith, however, the differences began to re-emerge. Until the seventh century the permission of the emperor was necessary for the election of a new pope. During the eighth, when the Eastern Church was troubled and divided by the iconoclastic controversy, the popes took advantage to dispense with this. Then the coronation of the barbarian Charlemagne in Rome in 800 as "emperor" by the Pope, in effect claiming to set up, on his own authority, a rival "Roman empire", was regarded in Constantinople as an act of profound treachery, both to the civilised world and the Christian faith.

Relations between the patriarchates of Constantinople and Rome further deteriorated when the Bulgar Khan Boris first accepted baptism from the Greeks, but was later persuaded to acknowledge the jurisdiction of the Pope, since he was more conveniently distant than the patriarch in Constantinople.

When Pope Nicholas tried to intervene in a quarrel within the Constantinopolitan Church over the legality of the election of the patriarch Photius, the entire empire, and Photius in particular, were outraged. A learned layman, Photius had been elevated to the patriarchate after his predecessor, Ignatius, had been deposed for barring the emperor from communion for incest. The deposed patriarch appealed to the pope, who supported his cause. Then in 866 Photius made the shocking discovery that churches under the jurisdiction of the Pope were using a form of the Nicene Creed which contained an unauthorised interpolation, stating that the Holy Spirit proceeded from the Father "and the Son". This added phrase, known by its Latin name, *Filioque,* had been introduced in Spain in the sixth century as a means of strengthening the anti-Arian position of the Spanish Church; this heresy still being particularly strong there at that time. When Charlemagne employed Spanish advisers at his court, this amended version of the Creed was introduced into the mass in his chapel at Aix. Since he always insisted upon uniformity as a matter of principle, the new usage spread widely, first throughout the Frankish Empire and then beyond it. Pope Leo had suggested that Charlemagne omit the offending phrase, but his advice went unheeded.

Thus Photius was not well disposed towards the pope for other reasons when he took up the cause of the Nicene Creed. He saw the interpolation not only as a corruption of the text by Frankish "barbarians" in the distant West, but as a weapon of anti-Byzantine propaganda among the Bulgarians. He denounced both Rome and the *filioque* clause, and summoned a council to Constantinople, where he denounced and excommunicated the Pope.

While he was about it, Photius threw in criticisms of several customs and practices peculiar to the West which had been introduced by Frankish missionaries into Bulgaria: opposition to a married priesthood, the reservation of the sacrament of confirmation to bishops, and fasting on Saturdays. This was directed at the fact that the missionaries were requiring from the newly-baptized Bulgarians complete abandonment of traditional Greek usages in favour of Roman ways. However, Photius did not consider mere diversity in practice and discipline as itself constituting a breach in the unity of the Church. The interpolation in the creed, and the heresy it implied, were the only doctrinal issues between them. This attitude was adopted by many of the theologians of Byzantium.

Since at that time the Papal court used a form of the mass which did not include the recitation of the creed at all, the Pope was not, strictly speaking, directly involved in the dispute. However, the attitude adopted at Rome during the controversy was that the Pope had the authority to do whatever he wanted. The long road to the declaration of Papal infallibility (1870) had begun.

A council of Eastern bishops held in 879-880, solemnly confirmed the original text of the creed and formally anathematized anyone who would either "compose another confession of faith" or corrupt the creed with "illegitimate words, or additions, or subtractions," Photius considered himself fully satisfied. To celebrate what he considered a final victory of Orthodoxy, he composed a detailed refutation of the doctrine of the "double procession".

Not surprisingly, it was Photius who took the Church in the area now called Greece from under the supervision of Rome, as part of the province of Eastern Illyricum, and placed it firmly under the jurisdiction of Constantinople.

The *Filioque* was later accepted in Rome itself when the creed was introduced into the mass there, probably in 1014, at the request of the emperor Henry II. After that, the issue was bound to be a matter of controversy during every subsequent encounter between Greeks and Latins.

Relations between the two Churches further deteriorated when the Normans invaded Southern Italy, an area under strong Greek influence. When a papal synod disallowed Greek usages in Italy, in retaliation Patriarch Michael Cerularius ordered the Latins in Constantinople to cease their own practices and adopt Greek ways. When they refused to conform, he closed their churches. In 1054 the pope sent the intransigent Cardinal Humbert to negotiate the differences between them. Disagreements about the *filioque* and the use of leavened or unleavened bread at the Eucharist were magnified rather than settled, and Humbert laid a papal bull of excommunication of the patriarch on the altar of Ayia Sophia, and walked out of the talks. Cerularius returned the compliment, leaving both bishops mutually excommunicated and in schism.

This event, known to history as the "Great Schism", has traditionally been seen as the final rupture between East and West. However, this was not seen at the time, when it must have appeared as just one more in a series of temporary breakdowns in a very stormy relationship. The Latin churches in Constantinople were gradually reopened and the temperature of relations was gradually lowered.

Meyendorff observed: "The schism which finally separated the Greek East and Latin West cannot be identified with any particular event or even be dated precisely. Political opposition between Byzantium and the Frankish Empire, gradual estrangement in thought and practice, divergent developments in both theology and ecclesiology, played their respective parts in this process."

But then a catastrophic adventure turned a breach of relations into a permanent rupture, accompanied by bad feelings which have not been entirely dissipated even today.

11

The Great Betrayal

The Catholic-Crusader Attack

The original Muslim tide which had swept across North Africa and Syria had been stayed by the Empire. But when a series of incompetent rulers ascended the throne, the health of the army was neglected, and a new threats sprang up on almost every frontier, disaster could not long be deferred. When the emperor Romanus IV faced an attack from the Seljuk Turks with an army which had been provided with neither pay, provisions nor equipment, which included cavalry regiments without horses and infantry regiments which paraded with pruning hooks, a major defeat was inevitable. At Manzikert, in 1071, the imperial forces were scattered by the Turks, and the emperor captured. The empire contrived to recover even from this disaster, but it had as a consequence of defeat lost its rich Anatolian provinces, which had supplied so many of its soldiers, and much of its food and revenue, and was considerably weakened. Yet despite the losses, the empire not only survived, it flourished, still effectively barring the way of an expansionist Islam into Europe. The bulwark of Christendom was shaken, but intact.

Then in 1204, taking advantage of a dynastic quarrel in Constantinople, a Western Crusader fleet heading ostensibly for Egypt was diverted by the Venetians to the City. Instead of strengthening the bastion of Christendom against Islam, they sacked it, and massacred many thousands of its inhabitants. During this outrage, the city was partly destroyed by fire during three days of indiscriminate massacre and plunder, which spared neither the treasures in the churches nor the ancient monuments in the public squares. A whore who had accompanied the Crusaders danced before the altar of *Ayia Sophia*, and later was installed upon the patriarchal throne. The chalices on the altars were used as drinking cups for drunken orgies. Ancient monuments were defaced. Most of the books in the City were burned. The total value of the booty taken at that time was thought to be equal to all the wealth of Western Europe combined. This included, for example, the four bronze horses, which were taken to adorn the cathedral of Saint Mark in Venice. These events, and the subsequent attempt by the Crusaders to impose the Roman form of Christianity upon the Eastern Empire by force, left a deep antipathy to Catholicism in the Greek world, which even today has not yet entirely disappeared.

It was not merely the riches of the City, but the empire, itself that was divided up among the looters, and a Latin emperor was enthroned. Count Baldwin of Flanders, was elected Emperor and received the Asiatic provinces. Boniface of Montferrat obtained

Thessaly and Macedonia, and his followers were allowed to establish themselves in Central Greece and the Morea. The Venetians took the islands of the Ionian Sea, the Cyclades, Aegina, Euboea, Acarnania, Aetolia, Adrianople and other possessions.

Pope Innocent III, who had not wished the diversion of the Crusade from its proper course, nevertheless decided to take full advantage of what had taken place. He demanded that the Roman Catholic Church be established as the official religion of the Empire; that the possessions of the Greek Church should be handed over to Latin clergy, and he appointed a Venetian as Patriarch of Constantinople. Many of the Latin rulers attempted to impose Latin clergy and Latin forms of worship upon the reluctant Greeks. The monks of Daphni Monastery, outside Athens, for example, were displaced to make way for Cistercians from the West.

By their treachery, the Venetians had succeeded in capturing the trade of the Eastern Mediterranean, but the Empire itself was destined to remain beyond their grasp. A Greek Emperor was left at Nicaea, and Greek despots controlled Epirus. As H. W. Davis observes, "The subject Greeks were not to be Latinised by a handful of energetic seigneurs and merchants."[1] One by one, the provinces of the Latin Empire were recovered: Adrianople and Thessaloniki in 1222, and the Asiatic territories by 1228. In 1261 the Greek emperor, Michael Palaeologus, finally re-entered his half-ruined capital. His dynasty was to retain the imperial throne until the fall of the City in 1453, although his empire was fatally maimed in its struggle to face down the growing onslaught of the Turks. Meanwhile in peninsular Greece and the islands, the Crusaders maintained their gains long after the disappearance of the Latin Empire; the Venetians and the Knights of St. John surviving longest.

The restored Greek emperor, Michael VIII, conscious of the now weakened state of his realm, sought reconciliation with the West to gain its support against the ever-present Turkish menace. Orthodox delegates attended a Council at Lyons in 1274 to discuss the healing of the schism between East and West. They were prevailed upon to accept both the supremacy of Rome and the *filioque*, but on their return to Constantinople, they could not gain the acquiescence of the citizens. The emperor's sister spoke for most when she said: "Better that my brother's empire should perish, than the purity of the Orthodox faith."[2] The Greeks of Thrace wrote to the Pope saying that the Latins could rule over the bodies, but not the souls of Greeks. An indication of how deeply the betrayal was felt is that the Greeks treated altars used by Latin priests as polluted, and rebaptized those first baptized by the Latins. Michael died a heretic and was buried in unconsecrated ground, and in 1283 his arrangements with Rome were repudiated.

Some western fiefs long remained in Latin hands, such as the Duchies of Athens and Naxos, while the Venetians for some time gradually extended their empire in the Aegean. Under their Latin rulers the Orthodox were sometimes mildly persecuted. But in some places, and for some long periods of time, the two faiths managed to coexist remarkably closely, even to the point of sharing church buildings, and taking part jointly in important celebrations.

Despite the Catholic occupation and persecution, and the ever-present danger from the Turks, the Greeks still contrived to generate another purely religious controversy among themselves. Mystical theologians in Byzantium had long favoured the language of light to

Mistra: The ruins of a Byzantine renaissance

The Emperor John Palaiologos travelling to the synod of Ferrara-Florence (1438)

describe the intense mystical experiences achieved by prayer. This light, they identified with the Uncreated Light of God, which the disciples saw when they witnessed the Transfiguration of Jesus on Mount Tabor, as recorded in the Gospel. This implies a direct experience of God, and therefore some first-hand knowledge of him. Yet the idea that a mortal could himself behold the Divine Light seemed incompatible with the dominant theology of the Eastern Church, expounded in works attributed to the Athenian disciple of Paul, Dionysios the Areopagite, which stressed that God is beyond all categories, and therefore beyond all experience, and ultimately unknowable. Those who supported the mystics, who were known as Hesychasts, were led by the archbishop, Gregory Palamas of Thessaloniki. He was opposed by a Greek monk from Italy named Barlaam the Calabrian, who argued that God can only be known indirectly. Gregory replied by distinguishing the "energies" of God from his "essence", arguing that what the mystic experienced was not the essence of God but his energies. God is known through his energies, by which he reveals himself to men. Barlaam also favoured union with Rome, and so he was opposed by the emperor, John VI Cantacuzene, the aristocracy, and the powerful monks of Mount Athos. With their support, the emperor was able to regain control of Thessaloniki.

Despite the shadow from the East, in the provincial capital of Mistra, overlooking the site of ancient Sparta, a succession of despots, usually a son or brother of the emperor, governed the Peloponnese. Here there flourished a revival of Byzantine learning and art which may have played a crucial role in the generation of the Italian renaissance, and hence, of the modern world.

During the mid fifteenth century the weakened empire, a pale shadow of its former power, saw in the growing might of the Turks the almost inevitable fate of the City. Emperor John VIII, the patriarch and a large delegation of clerics, travelled to the West to get help from fellow Christians to face the common threat at any price. At the Council of Florence of 1439, the terms proposed by the Pope proved once more to be to be submission to Rome and acceptance of the *filioque*, but with permission to continue Greek usages in worship. Resistance at home to this surrender was overwhelming, and when the emperor returned, he never dared issue an order enforcing the union.

When the city was hard pressed by Mehmet II, emperor Constantine XI appealed once more to the rest of Christendom for assistance. The Pope insisted that he promulgate the decree of union, which he dare not do, so no help came. Lucas Notaras, his army commander, declared that he would "rather see the Muslim turban in the midst of the City than the Latin mitre." The Greeks had learned much about the Roman Catholics during their lengthy attempts to suppress the Orthodox Church. In the end, when the long-awaited attack came, ironically, only a group of Venetian sailors appeared to help the Greeks with their ships, to be joined, equally ironically, by a contingent of rival Genoese.

After a two month siege by a force ten times that of the defenders, the clergy of both rites met together in *Ayia Sophia* for a final shared liturgy, and on the next day, Tuesday May 29th, the Turks breached the walls and the City fell. The mosaics of *Ayia Sophia* were covered in whitewash and the building was converted into a mosque.

Pope Pius II immediately sent a letter to Mehmet offering to "make him emperor" in return for his baptism: "Be baptized and no prince in the world will be your equal in glory and power. We will call you Emperor of the Greeks and of the Orient, and what you now possess by force and injury, you will hold by right. All Christians will venerate you, and make you the judge of their disputes... The see of Rome will love you like any Christian king, and so much the more as your position will be greater than theirs."[3] When that "long shot" failed, he at long last called for a new crusade to repel the Turks, a call which was universally ignored by Western leaders. In 1460 the Turks overran the Peloponnese, and in 1461 extinguished a "rump" Greek empire which had been set up at Trebizond, on the distant shores of the Black Sea.

12

The Centuries of Darkness

Under the Turk

Because the Greeks had been taught that they were the people of God's earthly kingdom whose ultimate victory over evil was certain, they seem to have been unable to reconcile themselves to what happened in 1453. The Turkish conquest was interpreted as a temporary punishment for the sins of the people, and as a divine intervention to prevent the subjugation of the Orthodox to the schismatic West and its Pope. It followed that one day, God would lead His chosen people out of captivity, restore to them all they had lost to Turk and Frank, and resurrect God kingdom on earth. In addition to the laments for the fall of the City, within a few years, songs were already being sung expressing hope for the recovery of the City and its Church of *Ayia Sophia*:

"They have taken the City, they have taken it, they have taken Thessaloniki,
They have taken the Holy Wisdom, the great cathedral
Which had three hundred altar-bells, and sixty-two great bells to chime.
For every bell there was a priest, for every priest a deacon...
But when Our Lady heard of this, she wept that the City had fallen.
Queen and Lady, do not weep, do not lament, but take comfort;
Some day, after years have gone past, once more the great Church shall be yours."

Another problem lay in the close relationship between emperor and Church in Byzantine thought. This is illustrated by an incident which had taken place in 1394, when the weakened empire was, as Romilly Jenkins points out, "less powerful by far than half a dozen city-states in Italy, and incomparably less powerful than France or England at that epoch." The Grand Prince of Moscow, Basil Dimitrievich, seems to have thought that a more realistic recognition of the political situation was overdue. He wrote to the Patriarch Antony that the Russians recognised the Orthodox faith, but could no longer recognise the emperor. "My son," wrote the patriarch in reply, "it is not well that you should say 'We have a church, but we have no emperor': for I tell you that it is not possible for a Christian to have church without emperor. Empire and church are a single unity, and to separate them is quite impossible. Thus "to pretend to be a Christian without loyalty to Christ's representative at Constantinople is rank hypocrisy, heresy and blasphemy." But now, the Orthodox Church was going to have to get along without a Christian emperor.

As Muslims, the Turks despised the non-Muslim peoples they conquered as "cattle". The latter were always liable to arbitrary treatment and mass deportation. They were

The Conquerors

subject to extensive and detailed discrimination, designed to make evident their inferiority. They had to dress differently from Turks. They could not bear arms or ride a horse. They could not build their houses higher than Turks. They paid special punitive taxes. But by far the most hated of the burdens of Turkish rule was that their sons were liable to be forcibly conscripted into the Sultan's army, where they would be brought up as Muslims, and their daughters forced into his harem. As "People of the Book," although distinguished from pagans, whom the Muslims believed they had a religious duty to exterminate, the Christians were spared this fate. But they could not build or repair churches, or even ring their church bells, without special permission. They were forbidden to marry Muslim women. It was death to attempt to convert a Muslim to Christianity, or for a Christian who had become a Muslim to revert to his previous faith. The ever-present possibility of sporadic violent persecution is evidenced by the many Neo-martyrs, those who lost their lives for their Christian faith under Turkish rule and who are now considered saints.

In general, the Turks confined their governmental activities to the minimum required to maintain control over their subjects. They levied taxes and controlled the army, provincial government and criminal justice. Apart from those things, they did not wish to get involved in the affairs of the conquered peoples. These were arranged in *millets* or communities, classified not by location but by religious affiliation. Within the empire, each *millet* was governed by a *millet basi*, who was the highest ranking religious dignitary within that community. All Orthodox Christians were regarded as part of the *Millet-I-Rum*, the largest of all the Ottoman millets, headed by the patriarch.

The patriarch and the church hierarchy were effectively co-opted into the Ottoman government. In return for their obedience and their taxes, and in return for securing the quiescence of their *millet*, they were allowed to govern the Orthodox community. The lay monk Skholarios, who had been enslaved by the Turks, was summarily emancipated, and promptly "elected" patriarch under the name Gennadius. He became an important agent of the Sultan, and was invested by him with his pastoral staff, in accordance with the ancient practice of the Byzantine emperors, using the words: "Be patriarch, preserve our friendship and receive all the privileges that the Patriarchs, your predecessors, possessed."

Turkish justice

The position of the patriarchs as having authority over the entire community of the Orthodox Christians was officially recognised. The patriarch could levy taxes and pass judgement.

In some ways, the more theologically distant, and disinterested, Sultan was an easier master than the emperors had been. Unlike the Christian emperors, the Sultan was unlikely to intervene directly in ecclesiastical or theological disputes. As the temporal ruler of the Orthodox *millet*, as far as the people were concerned, the patriarch now combined something of the roles of emperor and patriarch in himself, ruling over a state within a state.

In recognition of his new status, the Patriarchs adopted a mitre in the form of the imperial crown, had a carpet bearing the imperial eagle placed before their throne, and began to style their hair in the manner of the emperors. Ironically, it could be argued that the patriarchs of Constantinople were now doing what they had previously so untiringly complained about the popes of Rome, namely assuming the dignity, style, titles, and even the powers, of an absent Roman emperor.

The Church thus found itself in an ambiguous position. On the one hand, in its faith, worship, customs and practices, it preserved the cultural identity and traditions of the conquered people. On the other, it aided and abetted, and clearly profited from, collaboration with the invaders. Thus the Church for a long time encouraged submission to Turkish rule as

Left: metropolitan (Stackelberg, 1811)
Right: country priest from the neighbourhood of Thebes (Stackelberg, 1811)

a form of protection from the oppression of the Venetian Catholics.

As time passed, the Greeks began to win a pre-eminence position within the empire. Since the Turks considered commerce to be beneath their dignity, much of it passed into the hands of the Greeks. As subjects of the Sultan, the entire area of the Ottoman dominions was opened up to them, and at more advantageous terms than were available to the Italian trading states. In any case, Venice, the chief of these, was frequently at war with the Ottoman empire. In consequence the Greeks were able to acquire the reputation as traders throughout the Levant, together with the resulting wealth, foreign connections and foreign education.

Moreover, an essentially barbarous people, such as the Turks then were, could not govern a complex urban society, like Constantinople, by themselves, and Mehmet the Conqueror seems to have been aware of this from the beginning. The administrative skills of the conquered were needed by their new rulers. By the mid-seventeenth century, a clique of wealthy Greek families living near the Patriarchate in the Phanar, or "lighthouse" district of the City, came to monopolise certain high positions within the imperial administration.

Churches of old Athens

These included the very important offices of Dragoman of the Porte, or foreign minister; Dragoman of the Fleet (or *Capudan Pasha*), the head of the navy; *hospodar*, or governor, of Moldavia and Wallachia (now in Rumania); and others. Inevitably, the non-Greek-speaking Orthodox Christians within the empire, Rumanians, Bulgars and Serbs, came to identify the Greeks with their oppressors. This was to have grave consequences, both for the unity of the Orthodox Church, and for international relations in the Balkans, when those peoples later regained their independence.

During the centuries which followed, the growth of the Russian Empire in the north, largely at the expense of the Ottoman Turks, came to dominate Greek political thinking. The Russians began to regard their own state, now the leading Orthodox power in the world, as the successor state to the Byzantine Empire. Hence their rulers, the Grand Dukes of Muscovy, assumed the title of Caesar, or Czar (Tsar). Inevitably, the Russians came to appear as potential protectors and liberators of the Greeks. When, during a war between Russia and Turkey in 1770, the empress Catherine the Great sent the Orlov brothers with a fleet to incite a rising in the Peloponnese, the Greeks readily rose in rebellion. They received in aid only four ships, several hundred men and forty boxes of ammunition. In response, the Turks incited an Albanian invasion of the Peloponnese. The northerners wreaked havoc across the area for ten years, until they became such a general nuisance that the Turks themselves forced their withdrawal. By the early 1780s Catherine went so far as to propose a restored Byzantine Empire, but it was too late; by her earlier betrayal she had squandered for ever the possibility of Greek support.

One effect of this disaster, however, seems to have been to stimulate national feeling among the Greek educated classes, and a desire to throw off the Turkish yoke among the mass of the people, who had little to lose. During the late eighteenth century, something of an intellectual renaissance began to develop among Greeks. Traditionally, Orthodox Christians had resorted to the University of Padua, in the Venetian Republic, for their higher education. Thus an increasingly rationalist and materialistic ethos had influenced educated Greeks, who more and more looked back to Classical Greece to provide their national mythology and inspiration.

At the same time, acting for the Ottoman Government, the hierarchy inevitably attracted to themselves much of the odium which would otherwise have been directed towards the Turks. Bishop Theophilos of Kampania lamented, in 1788: "…in the days of the Christian empire, alas … prelates administered only the priesthood and ecclesiastical matters, and did not intervene in civil matters … Now, however, provincial prelates undertake secular lawsuits and trials in connection with inheritance, with debts, and with almost any aspect of Christian civil law." In addition, the people had to pay taxes to the bishop at Easter for marriages, ordinations and funerals. If any monk arrived seeking to collect alms, he first had to pay the bishop to obtain permission to beg.

The Patriarchs and the hierarchy also became deeply enmeshed in the all-pervading system of corruption which was characteristic of Ottoman Government. The Patriarch was theoretically chosen by the Synod, but the payment of a sum of money was required each time a patriarch was invested. The practice grew up that the would-be patriarch would purchase his "election" with I.O.U.s, and then, after he had been enthroned, he would demand that all the bishops contribute to pay off the sum he had promised for his preferment. The Bishops would demand this money from their inferior clergy, who, in their turn, would be forced to lay the burden upon the people. Moreover, since preferment had to be purchased, and since the Turkish government could depose a patriarch on a pretext provided by any single member of the Synod, it paid them handsomely to ensure a frequent succession of new appointments. In the eighteenth century, no less than forty-eight different men occupied the patriarchal throne over a period of sixty-three years. Since the bishops also had to purchase their promotion, they would, in their turn, do the same as the patriarch. In the end, these burdens would always fall upon the poor lay people.

Under these circumstances, it is hardly surprising that a spirit of anti-clericalism pervaded Greece during the years before independence. A British traveller, Sir William Gell, recorded "a saying common among the Greeks", that the country laboured under three curses, the priests, the *cogia bashis* and the Turks; "always placing the plagues in this order." Several travellers came across manuscript versions of an anticlerical poem composed by an Epirote, which was being circulated throughout Greece. It castigated the metropolitans as eating and drinking "like pigs", and "sleeping fourteen hours a night and two in the afternoon," and singing the liturgy twice a year. Asked why Greece was enslaved, a metropolitan replied: "I eat and drink with pleasure, I do not feel the tyranny... Two things I crave, yes indeed, by the icons, lots of money, and nice girls. Now as for Hellas, which you mention, it is of little concern to me if she has been tyrannised... We give them spiritual counsel to have faith in the ruler and respect the primate, not to regret giving money to the Turk."

Adamantios Korais believed that the salvation of the Greeks lay in achieving emancipation through education. The Church was the obvious source to look to for leadership. An eighteenth century revival led by Kosmas the Aetolian, a monk of Mount Athos, led to the foundation of over two hundred schools in northern Greece. However, Korais also found that the obscurantism of some of the clergy stood in the way of advance. A school founded on Mount Athos in 1753 had been forced to close down in 1759. An entire genre of books had been promulgated to counter the influence on the intelligentsia of liberal ideas from the West. Ceremonial book burnings took place frequently. In 1805 Beniamin Lesvios was condemned by the Patriarchate for the dreadful novelty of teaching that the

A Soul Saturdayin Athens Lithograph of C. F. Gille (1822)
(National Ethnological Museum, Athens)

earth orbited the sun. Korais had already spoken for the intelligentsia when wrote in 1788:
"...instead of a Miltiades and Themistocles, whom Europe still admires, we are governed by
scoundrels and stupid men as well as by an ignorant clergy who are even worse than our
foreign tyrants the Turks."

The monasteries were no more popular than the hierarchy. They did well under the
Turks. A good example is the Pendeli Monastery, founded in 1750 by Timothy, bishop of
Oropos, who, paradoxically, had fled his diocese because of persecution by the Turkish
Pasha. From nothing more than an abandoned monastic building, the community came to
acquire an area of land stretching across much of eastern Attica, from the borders of
Kifissia to distant Vraona. They acquired many privileges recognised in imperial *firmans*.
At the same time, they provided nine thousand pounds of honey annually to the Seraglio "as
a gift". According to Archimandrite Timothy Kilifis, "Turks respected monastic properties
but they plundered other properties every now and then." Generally, the monks were
attacked for living off alms from the poor; and were widely suspected of systematically
informing on the *kleftes* or brigands who harassed the Turks.

The spread of revolutionary sentiments was unwelcome to many in the Church
hierarchy. As Arnold Toynbee put it: "The Latin head-dress was not improved in Eastern
Orthodox clerical eyes when it was transmuted from the Pope's triple crown into the

133

sansculottes' Phrygian cap of liberty." In the fateful year 1789, an anonymous author, identified by some to be Patriarch Gregory V himself, published the *Paternal Teaching*, in which he condemned contemporary revolutionary ideas and praised the Sultan as the protector of Orthodox Christians, sent by God to save them from the Roman Catholics: "See how clearly our Lord, boundless in mercy and all-wise, has undertaken to guard once more the unsullied Holy and Orthodox faith of us, the pious, and to save all mankind. He raised out of nothing this powerful empire of the Ottomans, in the place of our Roman empire ... and He raised up the empire of the Ottomans higher than any other kingdom so as to show without doubt that it came about by divine will, and not by the power of man, and to assure all the faithful that in this way He deigned to bring about a great mystery, namely salvation to his chosen people... The all-mighty Lord ... puts into the heart of the sultan of these Ottomans an inclination to keep free the religious beliefs of our Orthodox faith and, as a work of supererogation, to protect them, even to the point of occasionally chastising Christians who deviate from their faith, that they have always before their eyes the fear of God." Some other hierarchs, however, such as bishop Ignatios of Arta, favoured national revolution, and had to flee the empire because of it.

The Struggle for Independence

During the winter of 1820 and 1821 acts of violence against Turks, the news of Ali Pasha's revolt, the intrigues of those plotting revolt, all contributed to a sense of crisis in the Peloponnese. The monks of Megaspelaion collected money for weapons. The primates of the Peloponnesus, who gathered the taxes, ran local affairs and acted as mediators with the Turks, were in debt to the Turkish government, and calculated that a revolt would both wipe clean their accounts and strengthen their ascendency in the districts they dominated. The higher clergy were sympathetic. In March, the Turkish authorities invited the Greek leaders to Tripolis to discuss the measures to be taken as a result of Ali Pasha's revolt. This alarmed them. Some of the primates and bishops decided to go; others believed it best to find some excuse not to attend. Bishop Germanos of Old Patras started out with his delegation on 18th March, but halted at Kalavrita, claiming he was ill. Clearly, revolution was in the air.

On March 17th revolt broke out at Areaopolis. On 23rd the Turks at Kalamata surrendered to Kolokotronis. On March 23rd they fled Vostitsa (Aigion), on the northern coast. As the news spread throughout the peninsula that the moment for the uprising had arrived, so the Greeks fell upon their Turkish neighbours. All over the Peloponnesus the Christians took up arms, as well as in Attica and Boeotia. The towns of Salona, Levadhia and Talenti in eastern Greece fell within the month, and the islands of Poros, Hydra and Spetses joined the revolt with their great resources of ships and sailors.

The Turks of Patras, meanwhile, had barricaded themselves into the citadel above the city when news of the insurrection reached them. On 25th March, Bishop Germanos gave the revolution its great symbol when he raised a banner with the cross on it at the monastery of Ayia Lavra,[1] and returned to Patras leading a band of a several hundred armed peasants. Preceding the army marched the clergy and monks, singing psalms and promising the crown of martyrdom to anyone losing his life in battle. When he arrived at the

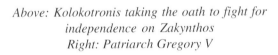
Above: Kolokotronis taking the oath to fight for independence on Zakynthos
Right: Patriarch Gregory V

port he celebrated the Liturgy, at which theose assembled swore an oath to deliver their country or perish, then the archbishop blessed the army. The French consul, reported that an icon of Christ was set up in the main square, and a cross erected above the Turkish mosques. That night the monks of Megaspelaion led the army in the prayer of the *Trisayion*. The independence struggle had, in some sense, become a crusade.

This revolt of his Christian subjects angered the Sultan Mahmud II, and the patriarch and Christians of Constantinople were to pay the price. On Saturday 10 April 1821, the patriarch officiated at the Liturgy preparatory to the Easter vigil in the church of *Ayios Georgios*. Ottoman forces surrounded the building, and, at its conclusion, pushed their way through the congregation seized the patriarch and the officiating bishops, dragged them into the courtyard outside, and tied nooses around their necks. The aged patriarch was then carried to the gate of the Phanar and hanged in his robes before his people. Because he was very thin, the weight of his body was not sufficient to cause instant death, and he suffered throughout the night. At the same time other bishops and priests were also seized and executed, including his ninety year old predecessor, Kyrillos, while others were imprisoned and later murdered. This attack provided the signal for a reign of terror against the Greeks in the City, which lasted for several weeks. Mobs broke into Greek churches and looted them. At one point fanatics broke into the patriarchate itself, those inside fleeing over the rooftops. The patriarchal throne and much of the property of the patriarchate was destroyed. The body of the Patriarch Gregory was left hanging at the gate for three days, so that anyone who entered had to push it aside, including his successor. Later, the Jews cut down the body, dragged the corpse by the legs through the streets down to the harbour,

135

weighted it, and threw it into the sea.

Meanwhile, eight bishops who had travelled to Tripolis were seized by the Turks and imprisoned: Kyrillos of Corinth, Chrysanthos of Monemvasia, Philotheos of Dhimitsana, Gregorios of Nauplion, Germanos of Christianoupolis, Philaretos of Olenos, Joseph of Androusa and Daniel of Tripolis. Of these five died while in prison; the others were freed when Tripolis was relieved by Greek forces in September 1821.

The nature of this revolt is not, in modern nationalist terms, a simple one. It seems to have been a rising of the Orthodox *millet* - of the Christian Orthodox subjects of the Porte. C. M.Woodhouse points out that most of the rebel leaders were, strictly speaking, non-Greek. Koundouriotis and other leaders of the Greek navy from Hydra and Spetses were Arvanites, descendants of Albanian settlers who had entered Greece during the Middle Age. Another, John Kolettis, was a Vlach, and the followers of Marko Botsaris were largely Albanian. By contrast, two of the leading "Turkish" commanders, Khurshid Pasha and Reshid Pasha (Kiutahi), were Orthodox Christians who had converted to Islam to further their ambitions in the Sultan's army. Moreover, those Greek islanders who were Roman Catholic in faith, on Syros, Tinos, Thira, and Naxos, descendants of Crusaders, Venetians and Frankish invaders, or their converts, tried to avoid any involvement in the war.

In the Peloponnesus, the bishops were often called upon to take the lead during the conflict, both in military and civil matters. Monks were also prominent in the struggle, particularly those of Megaspelion. Thus when independence was finally achieved, through the struggle of the freedom fighters and the *fiat* of the Great Powers, the leaders of the Church, despite centuries of active collaboration with the occupying power, could rightly claim to have conducted themselves honourably in the national cause. Many of the ordinary priests and monks were either martyred or fought bravely.

13

A Harsh Dawn

Just as, paradoxically, the fall of Constantinople had proved in some ways an unexpected advantage to the Orthodox Church, so, equally paradoxically, the achievement of independence turned out, in some ways to be a disaster.

Despite its long record of active collaboration with the Muslim conquerors, many among the hierarchy and monasteries had fought gallantly for independence. By the end of the war, some five hundred churches had been destroyed, and many monasteries forced to close. Many of the faithful had been killed, including bishops, priests and monks.

Despite the leading role many of these had taken in the struggle, freedom from the Turkish yoke brought with it a loss of many of the Church's traditional privileges. This was due to many factors: the weakening of the leadership of the Church during the war by losses and divisions; the imposition of a new foreign government, the Bavarian regency, by the Great Powers; the ambitions of the Greek primates, who did not wish to share power; and the hostility of many foreign-educated Greek intellectuals. Worse still, relations between the Church in free Greece and the mother Church of Constantinople were fractured. All this was made possible by a general attitude of passive acquiescence in moves against the Church by the new state and intelligentsia, by a general population, among whom the hierarchy and the monks were unpopular.

The Great Powers insisted that Greece be subject to a prince from one of the royal families of Europe. The population of the new kingdom was overwhelmingly Orthodox, as the Muslim Turks had either been killed in the war, fled, or were soon to leave. There were just a few Catholics on some of the Cyclades, and some Albanian Moslems. But when Capodistrias argued that the Greeks should have some say in the choice of a monarch, and that he must belong to the Orthodox faith, he was accused of coveting the post for himself. Since the Great Powers distrusted each other, and each wished to exclude the royal houses of the others, the Orthodox Romanovs, the royal family of Russia, were rendered ineligible. A Bavarian prince, Otho Wittlesbach, became king of Orthodox Greece. He never renounced his Roman Catholic faith, and he was later to marry a Protestant and make her queen. Thus newly-independent Orthodox Greece found itself saddled with a Catholic king and a Protestant queen.

Back in 1821 Adamantios Koraïs had publicised the idea of a church for a future Greek state independent of Constantinople. The influential Theoklitos Pharmakidis, a learned theologian who published the first newspaper in independent Greece, *The Greek Trumpet*, supported him and propagated the idea. In 1833, the National Assembly, meeting at Nauplion,

*Left: The arrival of King
Otho in Athens
1st December 1834
at the church of Saint
George, the Temple of
Theseus - Detail
(Peter von Hess,
New Gallery, Munich)*

*Opposite: King Otho and
Queen Amalia in the
Metropolis of Athens*

passed a law stating that "the Eastern Orthodox Church of Greece is dependent on no external authority, andspiritually owns no head but the Founder of the Christian Church." This proclamation asserted unequivocally the independence of the national Church of Greece, and made no reference whatsoever to the Ecumenical Patriarch. Thirty bishops whose sees lay inside the new kingdom signed it. To celebrate the new church Constitution, the Regency declared 27th July a holiday. An artillery salute opened the day, and in the cathedral, the members of the Synod took their oaths of office. On 25 July, the members of the Holy Synod, were announced. Theokletos Pharmakidis had been appointed its secretary. The new Synod sent a letter to the various churches of Greece, claiming that the Greek Church had been *de facto* autocephalous since 1821, and that the Constitution simply regularized this. When Metropolitan Kyrillos of Corinth, the President of the Synod, sent a letter to the patriarch in Constantinople explaining the situation, it was returned unopened.

One unforeseen long-term effect of this break from Constantinople was the precedent it set for the establishment of other, and rival, national churches in the Balkans, when other Christian communities achieved their independence.

By its new charter, no decision of the Synod was to be valid, or to be executed, unless signed by the government commissioner (procurator). The government of the Greek national Church had been placed very much in the hands of the state. This was a situation inherited from the Byzantine Empire and continued, in the face of *force majeur*, under the

Ottomans. But the Church of independent Greece had been effectively placed by the actions of its own citizens under the thumb of a government dominated by Bavarian Catholics.

There immediately followed a reform of the Greek Church modelled on those of Peter the Great in Russia, pushed through by the Bavarian regent Maurer. The building of further churches without permission was prohibited. Rules were laid down to control ordinations. Men from outside the kingdom were not to be ordained. Records of baptisms, weddings and funerals were to be kept.

The regents were well aware that the monks had been most vigorously opposed to the break with Constantinople, and that they were the most strenuous partisans of Russian influence in Greece, as they saw Russia as the leading Orthodox power in the world. So they moved vigorously against the monasteries. Under the Ottomans, much of the revenue of the religious houses had been used to support the relatives of the monks in residence. The government was resolved to expropriate this income for the state. The total number of monasteries was reduced to eighty-two. Rules were set up for the election of abbots. Administrative procedures were laid down, requiring regular reports of the number of monks in a monastery, their age, nationality and date of arrival; the property, income and expenses of the house. These reports were, as a matter of course, to be certified by the nomarch, and then sent to the Ministry of Religion. The celebration of baptisms and weddings in monasteries was forbidden. Attempts were also made to keep the monks inside their monasteries. Surplus monastic property was taken over by the government and sold for the benefit of the church. The convents of women, which were at that time generally very small, were ordered in 1834 to combine into three institutions, one in Attica, one in the Peloponnese and one for the islanders on Thira. If these houses were ever to have fewer than thirty nuns, they were to be closed down.

Despite the imposition of such measures by a foreign and Catholic government, popular feeling towards the monasteries remained hostile. In 1838 William Mure reported that in Elis they were commonly described as "hives of useless drones," and that the government measures were popular.

After a brief revolt, a constitution was granted by the king in 1844, which stated that the heir to the throne and all subsequent monarchs should be required to be Orthodox Christians. With the mediation of the Russians, a reconciliation was effected between the Greek national Church and the Patriarchate in 1850. The Patriarch recognised the independence of the Greek national Church, saving that all matters of theology should be submitted to the arbitration of Constantinople, and that the holy oil or chrism (*miron*) used in Greece should be requested from the Phanar. Following the resumption of relations, a new charter of 1852 enacted that "the Eastern Orthodox Church is and will continue to be the religion of the state, and that the state shall also appoint as many bishops and as many priests as necessary. The state will also make provision for their maintenance, and will also undertake the administration of Church property, such as the estates of the monasteries."

Unfortunately, the Greek state inherited the tradition of corruption inherent in the Ottoman administration. The Church became an integral part of the "patron-client" system which dominated the political and economic life of the country. This was most evident in the scandal called the *simoniaka* (1874-8), when two ministers in the government of Dimitrios Voulgaris were publicly accused of taking bribes from four clerics who wished to be nominated as bishops.

The nineteenth century was almost everywhere in Europe a time of increasing secularisation and marginalisation of religion. An intelligentsia developed in Greece, aided by the foundation of the University of Athens in 1837, which in part defined itself by a sceptical, and sometimes openly contemptuous, attitude towards the clergy and "popular superstitions". Many in this class went to study in Germany, and subsequently in France, where they became familiar with the free circulation of ideas incompatible with, or in opposition to, the Christian world-view.

Meanwhile, in the villages, the priest lost his position as leader and spokesman of the community, this role as village leader was taken over by elected representatives. Then with the arrival of schools, his role was reduced to a purely religious one.

The process of secularisation in other societies at this time frequently produced a reaction. Strongly anticlerical regimes in France and Portugal led to the establishment of pilgrimage cult centres at Lourdes and Fatima, respectively. In Greece a similar phenomenon was observed with the cult of the Virgin of Tinos. Several fundamentalist movements within the Church sought to stem the tide of secularism by the development of teaching movements, such as *Anaplasis*, founded in 1886, and the Brotherhood of Theologians, or Zoë, founded in 1907 by a monk of Megaspelaion. The latter was a society of celibate priests and laymen living under a common rule. During the post-war years many

Cathedral of Athens, mid-nineteenth century

other evangelical movements were fostered by the Zoë Brotherhood to renew the Church.

Despite immediate moves to reduce the power and influence of the Church after Independence, and despite the slow secularization of Greek society, it had always been intended, however, that the Orthodox Church would play a leading role in the new state.

Thomas W. Gallant points out that it was no accident that in 1838 the government chose to observe March 25th as the formal date of the outbreak of the revolution, and as a perpetual national holiday. The selection of this date focused attention upon the actions of archbishop Germanos at the monastery of *Ayia Lavra*, rather than upon lay leaders of the revolt in the south. At the same time, March 25th was the feast of the Annunciation of the conception of Christ to the Virgin.

In 1871, the Jubilee of independent Greece, a central part in the celebrations was the solemn translation of the body of Patriarch Gregory V from its resting place in Odessa to Athens. The remains were transported in a Greek warship named *Byzantion*. At Piraeus it was met by the entire hierarchy of the Greek Church and conveyed, accompanied by vast crowds, to Athens, where it was received by King George and Queen Olga, and interred in the new Cathedral. Alexander Kitreoff notes that "to associate the Patriarch with the commemoration of the Revolution was a decision laden with irony, because the Patriarch had excommunicated the leaders of the revolution in the Peloponnese upon hearing of the revolt in 1821."[1] Yet the intention to strengthen the bonds between state and Church was evident in this move.

The Church was occasionally able to employ the arm of the state to punish religious dissidence. Theofilos Kairis of Andros was condemned in 1839 for founding a new religion, *Theosevismos*, which attempted to reconcile rationalism and mysticism in a single system. He died in prison in 1853.

Moreover, reactionaries within the Church could occasionally wield great power. The language spoken by the people of Greece had evolved considerably from its ancient forms by the simplification of many grammatical structures and by the introduction of many words of foreign origin. Since the New Testament was always used in its original untranslated version in the churches, it was not readily comprehensible to the great mass of the people, and evangelical considerations called for a translation into the modern form of the language. In 1901 Queen Olga supervised a project, approved by the archbishop of Athens, to produce an authoritative translation of the Gospels into the Greek used by the mass of the people in their everyday life. This aroused violent opposition. It was argued that the translators were undermining the unique connection between Greek culture and the Gospel, as well as substituting an inferior version for the inspired original. This controversy resulted in a student takeover of the University and a protest meeting held among the columns of the Temple of Olympian Zeus. The government, which had forbidden the demonstration, ordered the Columns cleared, and soldiers fired blanks at the crowd. Serious riots led to eight deaths and over one hundred injuries, and there was an attempt on the life of the Prime Minister. The government, the chief of police and the archbishop of Athens all resigned, and the Holy Synod forbade the use of all translations. Today translations

Popular lithograph representing the Balkan League

of the text of the Bible may not be published without the prior approval of the Orthodox Church of Greece and of the Patriarch of Constantinople. This was not merely a religious issue. The university students had a vested interest in preserving the artificial form of the language, which only graduates understood, since it entrenched their privileged social and economic position. Nevertheless, this unusual union of the intelligentsia and reactionary elements within the Church had proved irresistible.

The Church also identified itself with the irredentist romantic nationalism which grew up during the nineteenth century centred around the "Great Idea" (*Megali Idea*), the liberation of all Hellenes outside the boundaries of the modern Greek state by incorporation into the kingdom, the recovery of Constantinople and the Byzantine Empire, and the establishment of the Greek king on the restored imperial throne and the Greek Patriarch to *Ayia Sophia*. Today it seems an absurd and quixotic idea, but in its day, it was no more so than the unification of Italy, which was achieved, or the creation of a "Greater Germany", which was managed for a brief period in the 1940s by Hitler.

As pressure on the Ottoman Empire to grant independence to its Christian subjects

Popular lithograph representing the "Great Idea"

increased during the nineteenth century, the Sultans tried to divide their Christian subjects along national lines, employing the old resentments of the non-Greek peoples of the privileges of the collaborator Phanariot Greeks. The key step in the implementation of this policy was the creation of a Bulgarian exarchate independent of the Ecumenical Patriarchate (1870). The effects of this policy were most keenly felt in the amorphous area of mixed peoples then known as Macedonia.

The result of these rivalries was that the "Great Idea", the reconstitution of a multinational empire, became distorted into a narrow nationalist dream of establishing a specifically Greek domination over the region, one likely to be resisted by all other groups. When he was archbishop of Drama, Chrysostomos Kalafatis characterised Patriarch Joachim III as "the most phoney" of the patriarchs for his attempts to retain the supranational role of the Orthodox Church, and heal the schism with the Bulgarian Church.[3]

Although there had been an independent state of Greece since 1830, most Greeks remained under Turkish rule in the late nineteenth century. The Cretans were especially restive, and there were several rebellions. Here the Church was wholly identified with the national struggle. The most noteworthy incident was the siege of the Arkadi Monastery in November 1866, when the abbot blew up the powder magazine, destroying the besieged rather than allow themselves to fall into the hands of the enemy, together with many of the besiegers.

The Church shared in the triumph of the state during the Balkan Wars of 1912-1913. Initially, with the formation of the Balkan League, for a short period, nationalist rivalries were put aside to liberate the rest of Europe from the Turks. Initially successful, fratricidal rivalries re-emerged and the Greeks forund themselves fighting the Bulgarians for disputed territory. nevertheless, extensive new lands were acquired by the Greek state in Macedonia, Epirus and Thrace.

The outbreak of the First World War exposed deep divisions within Greek society between those who, like the king, favoured the Central Powers, and those who, like prime minister Eleftherios Venizelos, favoured the Allies. The Church hierarchy allied itself firmly with the royal party, and appointment of bishops became a political football between the two groups.

Thus Greece was a divided nation, not at peace with itself when, in 1922, the Greek Army set out on an ill-fated expedition to realise the Great Idea by an attack upon Anatolia from its base in Smyrna. Instead of the recovery of Constantinople, their attack brought disaster upon the Greeks of that region, and a terrible martyrdom to Chrysostomos Kalafatis, then bishop of Smyrna. The settlement which followed in the Treaty of Lausanne, saw the end of the Great Idea with a massive exchange of populations between Greece and Turkey. At this time, the Church suffered a double blow. In addition to the shattering of the nationalist dream with which it had been closely associated, the defeat brought a new threat to the position of the Patriarchate with the rise of an aggressively nationalistic Turkish state.

A frequent response to crisis is to retreat into wholesale rejection of the modern. This is usually incompatible with the social and political ambitions of the hierarchy, and so leads to schism, as was the case with the Russian Old believers. A similar protest occurred with the adoption by Greece of the reformed calendar in 1924. Pope Gregory XIII had reformed the calendar by cutting out ten days from October 1582, and altering the number of leap years in a century. Most European nations adopted the reformed calendar relatively quickly, but three Orthodox Councils condemned the "Pope's calendar" as heretical. The Soviet Union converted to the Gregorian Calendar in 1918, following the Bolshevik Revolution. Then in 1923, Patriarch Meletios Metaxakis called upon all the Orthodox churches to adopt the change. Several agreed, including the Church of Greece, while others, including the monastic communities on Mount Athos, continued to adhere to the old calendar. The Greek Government, with the support of the Church authorities in Athens, introduced the reformed calendar in 1924. This reform caused a schism within the Greek Church, for some believers, who came to be known as "Old-Calendarists" refused to countenance the change. Despite the passage of time, and attempts by the authorities to suppress them, the Old Calendarists continue to resist change even today. It is not clear how many remain in schism, but they do have many monasteries, and maintain a hierarchy of their own, together with a network of parishes. However, they are divided among themselves over how to regard the official Orthodox Church. Some see it as a schismatic

*Archbishop Damaskinos
statue in the Cathedral Square,*

body, while others as one which no longer function as part of the True Church. Many Old Calendarists seem to have set themselves against any kind of adaptation to the modern world.

Although the kings of Greece were never able to dominate the Church, governments have routinely intervened to secure their own nominees in positions of importance. During the political upheavals which began with the National Schism in 1917, bishops were deposed and appointed according to whether they were supporters of King Constantine or Prime Minister Eleftherios Venizelos.

During the Occupation, however, during the Second World War, the Church of Greece found itself under the strong and capable leadership of arch-bishop Damaskinos, who acted as regent after the liberation. With the development of the Civil War and the American "protectorate", the Church sided unequivocally with the military, political and social establishment, alienating itself from the poor.

The Colonels, who seized power in 1967, regarded themselves as guardians of Orthodoxy as well as Hellenism. They sought to exercise this role by replacing the archbishop and synod with their own nominees, as well as by enforcing short hair for boys and long skirts for girls. They shame-lessly appropriated for their regime the language of religion, professing to seek to create "a Greece of Greek Christians," and sought to bring it about using arbitrary arrest, labour camps, and the torture of prisoners. One effect of this was to further compromise the Church in the eyes of many citizens.

Meanwhile the Greek population of Constantinople has been systematically eroded. Its position was safeguarded by the Treaty of Lausanne, as was that of the Turks of Thrace. But since that time, the Turkish population of Thrace has grown, while the Greeks of Constantinople have been forced out by discrimination and violence. Much of the Phanar Quarter has been resettled by Kurdish refugees since government-instigated riots in 1956, when three quarters of all the Greek churches in Constantinople were attacked and sacked in a single night, and most of the Greeks were driven out of the country. By means of a law requiring that the ecumenical patriarch must be a citizen of Turkey, the Turks have attempted deliberately and systematically to deprive the patriarchate of the means of survival. The famous Theological School of Halki, chief source of priests for the territories directly under the jurisdiction of the Patriarchate, has been closed by the Turks in a transparent attempt to impair its leadership, by cutting off the pool of available talent.

14

The Contemporary Challenge

After its early triumphs, the story of Orthodoxy in its Greek manifestation is one of repeated loss and tragedy. Given the Orthodox world view developed in Constantinople, these losses are, on the face of it, inexplicable, and they set up a certain psychological tension. This can most immediately and easily be absorbed by adopting a defensive stance towards the world.

At the beginning of the twenty-first century the ecumenical patriarchate is still being deliberately and systematically deprived of the means of survival by the Turkish authorities. This is clearly illustrated by the life-story of the present patriarch, Bartholomaios, who comes from Imbros, formerly a Greek island, but now massively repopulated with Turkish settlers. With the Theological School of Halki closed by the Turkish government, and the requirement that the Patriarch be a Turkish citizen, the supply of priests must in time dry up, and the Patriarchate in this way will be strangled. This is not a result of pressure from Islamic fundamentalists; it is due to the planning of the Turkish military, political and business establishment, which has always been hostile to Hellenism.

To many, the long-term position of the Patriarchate within Turkey seems impossible, and its transference to Thessaloniki or Mount Athos has been proposed on several occasions. But the present state of Turkey has clearly exposed the bankruptcy of that country's ruling "elite", whose only trump card, up to the Iraq War, was a servile conformity to every demand of successive US administrations. Manifestly corrupt and incompetent, they are unpopular in their own country. Desirous of entry into Europe, they are yet unwilling to accept the terms of entry, including the establishment of the rule of law, and a genuine democracy, with only a back seat for the military and respect for human rights; all of which would inevitably spell their demise. The Patriarchate may yet outlive them.

In Greece proper, the situation appears more positive. The position of the Greek national Church as the "dominant" religion according to the Constitution is a privileged one. The Church receives subsidies from the Government in addition to clergy salaries paid by the state. It is the largest landowner in the country. The teaching of the Orthodox religion is compulsory at all levels of education, and the requirement of the Church's prior approval for the building or repairing any non-Orthodox place of worship demonstrates its entrenched privileged position. A Greek citizen can allow his children to opt out of religious education, but only if he or she explains the reasons for it; that is, demonstrates in public, a non-Orthodox religious identity, inviting discrimination.

The hierarchy of the National Church has long viewed itself as the guardian of the Greek national identity, and at present resists all those tendencies which make Greeks more European and less Greek, while Greek nationalists use the Orthodox Church to buttress the Hellenic national identity.

Yet there is much to cause concern. Attendance at the normal Sunday Liturgy in Greece has been estimated at only five per cent of the population, equal to that of the United Kingdom. Church attendance *appears* to be greater because in Greece the vast majority of churchgoers attend the services of a single Church, and are not divided among various denominations. However, this figure is not as significant as it would be in the West. Greeks are not required to attend church on each Sunday in the way that Roman Catholics are. Moreover, the Greeks' greater sense of community leads them to consider that even if an individual is not personally present, he or she is part of the wider community which *is* offering worship. Sometimes one member of the family, usually the mother, is considered as the representative of the entire family when she attends church.

Moreover, the seasonal observances of the Church are both profoundly enjoyed and totally unassailable. Attendance at the special ceremonies which mark the different seasons of the year is impressive. Almost no one voluntarily misses the service of Resurrection at Easter. But many among the educated middle classes in Athens take a perverse pride in never actually entering the building, which is always full at that time anyway, and in arriving as late as possible before midnight and leaving as early as possible afterwards. Moreover, for many people, these occasions are regarded affectionately as folk observances which everyone would be the poorer for losing, rather than as essentially religious in character.

In addition, the Old Calendarist schism remains, so that many of the monks, nuns and laity, including a disproportionate number of the most committed, remain in schism.

The increasing distance of the laity from the Church has many causes. Many have been alienated by the association of the hierarchy with the political right, and by the power and influence over national life which the bishops wield. Others feel that religious faith is incompatible with a modern scientific world-view. But for most, it seems to be a matter of life-style. Regular attendance at church and deference towards the clergy is associated by many urban or urbanised Greeks with a way of life characteristic of "the village"; and of a way of life regarded as poor, uncomfortable and backward, from which they have but recently escaped. For Westerners, the rural life we have collectively left behind is seen through a rosy glow. For urban Greeks the move into the towns was so recent that they are still relieved to have escaped the cold, damp, dirt, boredom, limited horizons and sheer hard work of the old way of life for their centrally heated, easily cleaned apartments, televisions, refrigerators and cars.

During the mid 1990s, Prime Minister Andreas Papanandreu threatened to separate Church and state, and to confiscate Church lands. The Church, which regards all actions taken against its resources as blasphemous attacks upon God and true religion, threatened government ministers acting contrary to its interests with excommunication. Amidst scenes reminiscent of medieval Constantinople, priests, monks and zealots from all over the country poured into the streets of Athens brandishing banners,crosses and icons, and holding prayer vigils outside Parliament. The government retreated.

Under the leadership of the populist archbishop Christodoulos, the hierarchy seems to have adopted a highly politicised approach towards challenges. Probably the first archbishop to be chosen in an election not influenced by the government of the day, in his initial "keynote" sermon, he immediately sounded an alarm against "europeanisation". In the face of this unwelcome clerical interference in politics, both the President of the Republic and the Prime Minister (representing different wings of the political spectrum) declined to attend his enthronement ceremony. Since that time there have been a series of crises in Church-State relations.

*A Greek church displaying
national flags during a holiday*

An invitation to Pope John-Paul II by President Kostis Stephanopoulos, in response to the pope's long-standing desire to visit the Greek capital to retrace the journeys of the apostle Paul, aroused initial opposition. There is little understanding among the Greek laity of how little, in terms of belief, actually divides their church from that of the Roman Catholics. Instead, there remains a deep-seated antagonism, which is perpetually fanned by sections of the monks and the hierarchy. The priest's trade union, which represents about 8,000 married priests, described the Pope as "the two-horned grotesque monster of Rome."[1] Archbishop Christodoulos asserted that he would greet the Pope "by bringing to his attention - with frankness, clarity as well as with theological and historical documentation - all of those dogmatic, ecclesiastical and historical issues that provoke sadness, bitterness and intense concern among the Orthodox world..." Nevertheless, the visit took place, and since that time there seems to have been something of a mild thaw in inter-Church relations.

In the same year a dispute started in Greece over the content of the national identity cards which all Greeks must carry with them at all times in public places. The Authority for Protection of Personal Data ruled that the bearers' religion should not be published on the card. This was necessary in order to conform to the European Union's standards on privacy protection and civil rights. Brushing aside a demand from Archbishop Christodoulos that the issue be put to a referendum, Prime Minister Costas Simitis announced on July 17th that the cards would no longer specify religion, occupation, spouse's name, or thumbprint.

Leaders of Jewish, Muslim, Roman Catholic, and other minority faith groups in Greece expressed support for the government decision, which they felt would help reduce discrimination. It was pointed out at this time that the practice had been initiated by the Nazi Occupation Authorities during the Second World War, in order to identify Jews for deportation. Human rights groups were also supportive, alleging the existence of systematic discrimination against non-Orthodox in Greece today, particularly in the award of jobs in the

Protesting clerics on the march against the new identity card

civil service. However, the proposed reform was vigorously opposed by the Church, and by many conservative politicians.

Huge rallies were organized by the Church, in which hundreds of thousands took part. One reporter wrote: "Greece is experiencing a profound identity crisis as it wrestles with what it means to be Greek, and how Greek traditions fit in with the rest of Europe."[3] A petition to demonstrate citizens' opposition to the government was organised. It was claimed that priests pressed mourners at funerals, guests at baptisms and weddings, and worshippers at the Liturgy to join the "crusade". By August 2001, more than three million Greeks had signed. The Church then repeated its demand for a referendum, but the Government argued that this was not appropriate when basic human rights were involved. A poll conducted in mid-2000 by *Eleftherotypia*, a national daily newspaper, found that 46% of respondents opposed the elimination of religious data on the ID cards, almost 40% favoured it, while 14% were undecided.

There is also some discontent among the ranks of the clergy themselves. In 2002 some Greek priests petitioned to be able to travel in public without their long black robes and pipe hats, and to shave their beards, in order to modernize their image, increase their marriage prospects, and enable them to reach out better to ordinary people. The church rejected the request.

Increasing openness in society threatens the standard account of the part played by the Church in the history of the nation. There are signs of an increasing willingness to examine the past in a more open and objective manner, and this includes the role of the Church. A team of professors from the University of Crete recently published a scholarly study on the myth of the "Secret Schools". According to the popular account, during the centuries that preceded the War of Independence, Greeks were forbidden to learn their own language and history, in order to make it easier for the Turks to assimilate the Greek population of their Empire. According to the legend, assiduously propagated by the Church, the clergy and monks set up and operated "secret schools" in caves and cellars to keep the national identity alive. In this study, it was demonstrated that the "Secret Schools" were a myth which served as an alibi for the Church's collaboration with the Ottoman authorities. Characteristically, the study was criticized not on the basis of any specific scholarly short-comings, but because of the authors' alleged "anti-Hellenism".

One hundred years ago, Adrian Fortescue wrote: "Nothing in the world is more dead than the Empire that fell with Constantine XII, and yet its ghost still lingers around the Byzantine altars." This is no less true today. A sense of the fustiness of their Church some-times overcomes Greeks, who say that Christ is tired of the repeated chant of *Kyrie eleison;* a projection, surely, of their own feelings. The fortress mentality of the current leadership can do nothing to ease that situation, and in time it will grow worse.

At the same time, Greeks have entered enthusiastically into the consumer society. The chief preoccupation of many is with the false world created by the media. Their goals are improved material living standards. This, grafted onto traditional attitudes which grew up during centuries of oppression and exploitation, which value "cleverness", successful dishonesty, and the "collective selfishness of the family unit", and which sees the public world and the state primarily as a souce of plunder, has led to a collapse of traditional morality. Yet the National Church seems to be indifferent towards, and even oblivious to this, and in no way can it claim to exercise any moral leadership. A force for unthinking moral conservatism, tainted by its incorporation into an essentially corrupt system of public life, its role seems to be largely restricted to politics: the defence of its privileges, and the generation of potentially dangerous nationalist sentiment.

Despite all this, the future of the Greek Church seems by no means as bleak as that of many other comparable religious bodies. In many countries, adherence to the church of the majority is by default, something which could easily be changed by an act of choice. Yet in over fifteen years I have never met a Greek for whom this was a genuine option.

It is not so much that Greeks choose to remain faithful to their Church by conscious preference. It is rather that the possibility of making a choice at all never enters their mental horizons. However ignorant or sceptical they may be about the doctrines of their Church, however cynical about the motives and behaviour of its clergy, however patronising their stance towards more devout relatives and neighbours, however infrequently they them-selves darken the doors of a church, the possibility of a change of religious affiliation never enters their minds. Being Christian Orthodox is an essential, and therefore an unquestioned, part of their identity. They will be married by a Greek priest; their children will be baptised in a Greek Church; and at midnight on Easter Day each year they will be found standing outside a church holding a lighted candle, waiting to hear the annual proclamation that "Christ has risen!"

Glossary

aer – a veil placed over the sacred vessels, the chalice and paten, used during the liturgy

anathema – a solemn curse on laid upon heretics by the Church

antidoron – blessed bread which is distributed at the end of the liturgy as a substitute for taking communion

archimandrite – an honorific title for an unmarried priest-monk of distinction, originally an abbot of a monastery of distinction

acolyte - altar server

apse - the projecting part of a building, usually semicircular

Arians – followers of Arius, heretics who believed that Christ was sent by god and superhuman, but not divine

ascetic - one who lives a life of extraordinary privation for religious motives

azymos – unleavened bread

bema – the chancel, the eastern portion of the church behind the image screen

caloyer – a monk

catechumens – those under instruction preparing for baptism

chasuble – the Western name for the outer vestment of the priest at the liturgy, a circular mantle with a hole through which he puts his head, which falls to the ankles except at the front, where it is cut away at the elbows.

chrismation – the sacrament of confirmation

Christology - doctrine about the nature of Christ

chrysobul - a formal decree of a Byzantine emperor

diakonikon –the part of the church where the priests and deacons put on their vestments

diaspora – Greek Orthodox Christians living outside Greece, i.e. in the UK, Australia, Canada or USA

diskos – the small flat plate upon which the holy bread is placed at the eucharist, the paten

epanokalymmafkion - the cylindrical hat of a senior cleric, with a veil

epistasia - the governing committee of the Holy Mountain

eschatology - doctrine about the" last things": death, judgement, hell and heaven

euchologion - book containing the ritual for administering the sacraments

filioque – the clause "and the son" added to the Nicene Creed in the Western Church and not recognised by the Othodox

Great Entrance – the procession which begins the Liturgy of the Faithful, in which the sacred vessels containing the bread and wine are born aloft, the offertory procession

hegoumenos – an abbot

heresy – "incorrect or false belief"

Hesychasts – mystical theologians who believed in the possibility of a physical vision of the Uncreated Light of God

hierodeacon – a deacon-monk

hierokeryx – a licensed preacher

hieromonk – a priest-monk

iconoclast – someone who is against the veneration of religious images

iconodule – someone who is in favour of the veneration of religious images

iconostasis – the screen which divides the nave of a church from the sanctuary, which bears the icons

igoumenos – an abbot

kalymmafkion – the cylindrical hat of a cleric

kellia - the cells of a monastery

koinobion – a monastery in which the monks share a common life

koinotia - the governing body of the Holy Mountain

Latins – Roman Catholics, from the language used in their liturgy

litany – a series of prayers recited by the deacon, to which there are responses sung by the cantors

Little Entrance – the procession which begins the Liturgy of the Catechumens, in which the Book of the Gospels is born aloft

metropolitan – diocesan bishop

millet – a community within the Ottoman empire, subject to the *Sultan*, but governed by the heads of its own community under its own laws

Monophysites – followers of the Alexandrian theologians, heretics who believed that Christ, although both God and man, possessed a single nature

Monothelitism – an attempted compromise between Orthodoxy and Monophysitism, favoured by some Byzantine emperors as a means of securing the unity of the empire

mosaic - a design made by inlaying small pieces of stone or glass of different colours

mystery religion - ancient religion in which a process of initiation after a period of preparation led to the revelation of "mysteries" concealed from those outside the faith

name day – the day of the saint or mystery whose name a person bears as his/her Christian name

nave – that part of the church occupied by the congregation

Nestorians – followers of Nestorius, heretics who held that Christ was a man into whom the Spitrit of God entered, but his mother could not be called the Mother of God

old calendarists – Orthodox who have refused to accept the implementation of the Gregorian calendar

orthodoxy – "correct belief"

orthros – the office of the dawn, lauds

Panayia – the all-holy One, the normal mode of referring to the Virgin Mary

paniyiri – a festival or celebration, especially the patronal festival of a church or chapel

Pantokrator – Christ as the ruler of all things, the Almighty

papas – a married priest

pnefmatikos – a confessor

primates - the lay leaders of the Greek communities of the Peloponnese

prosphora – the eucharistic bread

protoepistates - the president of the governing committee of the Holy Mountain

prothesis – the preparation of the bread and wine before the liturgy; the part of a church where this takes place

protodeacon – an honorific title for a deacon of distinction

protopapas – an honorific title given to a married priest of distinction

psaltes – a singer or cantor

sanctuary – the central space behind the altar screen, frequently semi-circular, where the altar
   stands

schism – a division within the Church

semandron – a plank of wood (or more rarely a strip of metal), either hanging suspended or carried
   on the shoulder and struck with a mallet to summon monks to church

skete – a dependent monastery, or "daughter house" of a monastery

skoufos – the head-dress of a monk

stauropegia - monasteries which are directly under the jurisdiction of the ecumenical patriarch and
   independent of the local bishop

Theotokos –Mary, the Mother of God

unction - rite of anointing the sick

Uniates – Members of the Roman Catholic Church descended from Orthodox or other Eastern
   Christians, who joined the Catholic Church *en masse*, and who were allowed to retain their
   distinctive ritual and customs, e.g. married priests and the use of unleavened bread,
   during the liturgy.

References

Preface
[1] Hammond, 19.
[2] Toynbee, 96.

1. Temples of Gold
[1] Stewart, 20.
[2] Toynbee, 112-3.
[3] Mayfield, Guy, 7.

3. Heaven on Earth
[1] Toynbee, 99.
[2] Ware, Timothy, 269.

5. The Annual Drama of Salvation
[1] Hammond, 51-2.

7. Black Angels
[1] Quoted in Johnson, Paul *A History of Christianity*, (London, 1976) 97.
[2] Choukas, 61.
[3] Choukas, 61-2.
[4] Choukas, 62.
[5] Tsiakos, T & Sakellaropoulos, S, *Ta Monasteria tis Attikis*, (Athens, 1995) *passim*.

8. The Faith Received from the Apostles
[1] Fortesque, 361.
[2] Meyendorf, 92.
[3] Hammond, 15.

9. The Great Synthesis
[1] There has been some controversy over theories that the Gospel of Matthew was originally written in Hebrew, but this is not generally accepted by scholars today.
[2] Sophocles 1
[3] Toynbee, 96.
[4] Toynbee, 95.
[5] Hore, 2.
[6] Hore, 1.
[7] Hore, 1.
[8] Quoted in Williams, Charles, *The Descent of the Dove*, (London, 1939) 21.

10. The Realm of Light

[1] Williams, 48.
[2] Southern, 53.
[3] Runciman, , 119.
[4] Johnson, 184.
[5] Southern, 54.
[6] Meyendorff, 92.
[7] Meyendorff, 92.
[8] Diner, 48-9.
[9] Diner, 85.
[10] Diner, 51.

11. The Great Betrayal

[1] Davis, 154.
[2] Quoted in Ware, Timothy, 71.
[3] Quoted in Southern, 89.

13. A Harsh Dawn

[1] Quoted in Gallant, 69.
[2] Quoted in Makridis, 190.

14. The Contemporary Challenge

[1] Patrick Quin, Athens, Greece, 07.03. Associated Press.
[2] Athens News Agency.
[3] Anthee Carassava, "Greeks debate privacy rights vs. religious identity," *Christian Science Monitor,* 22.06.00 p7.

Bibliography

The Orthodox Church

Adeny, W.F., *The Greek and Eastern Churches*, (Edinburgh, 1908)

Andrews, T., *The Eastern Church*, (New York, 1957)

Botsis, Peter A., *What is Orthodoxy?* (Athens, n.d.)

Callinikos, The Rev. Constantine, *The Greek Orthodox Church*, (London, 1918)

Fortescue, Adrian, *The Orthodox Eastern Church*, (London, 1907)

French, R.M., *The Eastern Orthodox Church*, (London, 1951)

Hammond, Peter, *The Waters of Marah: The Present State of the Greek Church*, (London, 1956)

Littledale, The Rev. Dr., *The Holy Eastern Church: A popular outline of its history, doctrines, liturgies and vestments by a priest of the English Church*, 2nd ed. (London, 1873)

Sophocles, S.M, *The Religion of Modern Greece*, Institute of Balkan Studies, (Thessaloniki 1961)

Theodorou, Evangelos D., *The Church of Greece*, (Athens, 1959)

Waddington, George, *The Condition and Prospects of the Greek or Oriental Church*, (London, 1854)

Ware, Kallistos, *The Orthodox Church,* (London, 1963)

Zernov, Nicolas, *The Church of the Eastern Christians*, (London, 1942)

Theology

Gavin, F., *Some Aspects of Contemporary Greek Orthodox Thought*, (London, 1923)

Lossky, V., *The Mystical Theology of the Eastern Church*, (London, 1957)

Meyendorff, John, *Byzantine Theology: Historical Trends and Doctrinal Themes*, (London & Oxford, 1974)

Monasticism

Byron, Robert, *The Station, Athos: Treasures and Men* (London, 1928)

Cavarnos, Constantine, *Anchored in God*, (Athens, 1959)

Choukas, Michael, *Black Angels of Athos*, (London, 1935)

Dawkins, R.M., *The Monks of Athos* (London, 1936)

Kadas, Sotiris, *Mount Athos* (Athens, 1979)

Kaestner, Erhart, *Mount Athos: The Call from Sleep* (London, 1961)

Simonpetritis, Andrew, *Holy Mountain: Bulwark of Orthodoxy and of the Greek Nation* (Thessaloniki, nd)

Icons

Ouspensky, Leonid, *Theology of the Icon*, (New York, 1978)

Robinson, Stuart I., *Images of Byzantium: Learning about Icons*, (London, 1996)

Talbot Rice, D., *Byzantine Art*, (London, 1935)

Worship

Elias, The Rev. Nicholas, *The Divine Liturgy Explained*, 4th ed. (Athens, 1979)
Hamilton, Mary, *Greek Saints and Their Festivals*, (Edinburgh & London, 1910)
Mayfield, Guy, *An Anglican Guide to the Orthodox Liturgy*, (London, 1962)
Papoutsis, Carole, *The Festivals of Greek Easter*, (Athens, 1982)

History

Clogg, Richard, "Anticlericalism in Pre-Independence Greece," in *Studies in Church History*, ed.
 Derek Barker *13*, (1976) 257-277
Diner, Helen, *Emperors, Angels and Eunuchs: The Thousand Years of the Byzantine Empire*, Tr.
 Eden & Cedar Paul, (London, 1938)
Every, G., *The Byzantine Patriarchate*, (London, 1947)
Frazee, Charles A., *The Orthodox Church and Independent Greece 1821-1852*, (Cambridge, 1969)
Gallant, Thomas W., *Modern Greece*, (London, 2001)
Hore, The Rev. A.H., *Eighteen Centuries of the Orthodox Greek Church*, (London, 1899)
Makrides, Vasilios N., "Secularization and the Greek Orthodox Church in the Reign of King George
 I," in *Greek Society in the Making 1863-1913: Realities, Symbols and Visions*, ed. Philip
 Carabott, (Aldershot,) 179-196
Meinardus, Otto F.A., *St. Paul in Greece* (Athens, 1972)
Papadopoulos, Theodore H., *Studies and Documents relating to the History of the Greek People
 under Turkish Domination*, (Brussels, 1952)
Prodromou, Elisabeth, "Democratization and Religious Transformation in Greece: An
 Underappreciated Theoretical and Empirical Primer," in *The Orthodox Church in a
 Changing World*, eds. P. Kitromilides & Th. Veremis, Hellenic Foundation for European
 and Foreign Policy: Centre fore Asia Minor Studies (Athens, 1998) 99-154
Runciman, Steven, *Byzantine Civilisation*, (London, 1933)
Toynbee, Arnold, *The Greeks and their Heritages*, (Oxford, 1981)

General

Davis, H.W.C., Medieval Europe, 2nd ed. (London, 1960)
Southern, R.W., *Western Society and the Church in the Middle Ages*, (London, 1970)

Other *Anagnosis* books about Greece by John L. Tomkinson

Travellers' Greece: Memories of an Enchanted Land

Price 32 euro
ISBN - 960-87186-4-3
Paperback
608 pages
61 illustrations (b&w)

Extracts from over one hundred writers
spanning more than three centuries!

"[A] comprehensive and extensive anthology of travel writing, comprising the views and impressions of over one hundred visitors to Greece, spanning a period of more than three centuries (from the late 16th to the early 20th). Illustrated with beautiful artworks depicting the most characteristic Greek landscapes and monuments (old prints, lithographs, sketches and paintings by foreign artists which have been reproduced in black-and- white, this is certainly a well researched book which displays how this land has enchanted and angered many with its (for them) peculiar and exotic ways of life…

"The anthology comprises some rare and now difficult to access works. The names you will come across might not be the most familiar (from the Rev Rufus Anderson, a clergyman visiting in 1828, to Chateaubriand, a Breton army officer and Dr. Corrigan, physician of the Queen in Ireland), but this is exactly what makes this book interesting research." *Athens News*

"Whether it is the American poet N. Parker Willis perturbed by the sight of British soldiers on Corfu in 1850, or Sir Kenelm Digby filching marbles while on a naval campaign to harass the Turks in 1727, there's plenty to delight and enrage here.... it is certain that many will be inspired to consult the original works." *Kathimerini* (English Edition)

GREECE BEYOND THE GUIDEBOOKS

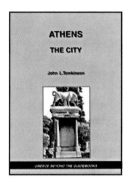
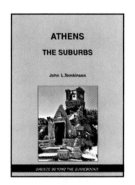
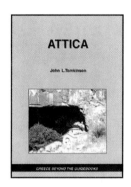

1. Athens: The City (ISBN 960-87186-0-0)
Stories from the city centre, and the districts of Plaka, Psiri, Metaxurgio, Votanikos, etc.

2. Athens: The Suburbs (ISBN 960-87186-1-9)
Stories from Kifissia, Maroussi, Filothei, Pendeli, Halandri, Kokkinia, Piraeus, Faliron, Nea Smyrni, Papagou, Kaisariani, Glyfada, Voula, Vouliagmeni, etc.

3. Attica (ISBN 960-87186-2-7)
Stories from Elefsina, Acharnon, Mount Parnes, Tatoi, Dionysos, Mount Pendeli, Mount Hymmettos, Pallene, Pikermi, Vraona, Mount Lavrio, Sounio, etc.

Price 15 euro each, paperback, 160 pages, illustrated (b&w)

Greece beyond the Guidebooks will provide you with "plenty of reading material around all this ancient region's archaeological wonders and other impressive monuments, without failing to make your read an interesting one," including "that extra … information on sites, villages and their history." Each volume "doesn't neglect to inform you of a region's lesser known monuments." *Athens News*

"They are the kind of books that may remind you of your favorite history teacher, the one who told you the interesting and strange pieces of history that the text books left out. From close encounters of the third kind to little-known temples, haunted villas, secret schools and teachings and even stories of Jesus walking in Attica in the 1930's." Matt Barrett

In preparation: **4.** *The Saronic Gulf* **5.** *The Isthmus: Corinth and Megara*

Stories the guidebooks do not tell
Sites the guidebooks overlook

For up-to-date information on all Anagnosis books,

visit our website: **www.anagnosis.gr**

fax: ++30-210-62-54-654

email: anagnosis@anagnosis.gr

telephone: 0030-210-62-54-654

Harilaou Trikoupi 130, Kifissia, 14563 Athens, Greece